DEPARTMENT OF HEALTH

An Introduction to The Children Act 1989

A NEW FRAMEWORK FOR THE CARE
AND UPBRINGING OF CHILDREN

LONDON: HMSO

© Crown copyright 1989

First published 1989

Sixth impression 1992

ISBN 0 11 321254 2

Since the first printing of 'An Introduction to the Children Act 1989', the following publications, aimed principally at professionals and agencies for the Personal Social Services and Health Service, have been issued and are available from HMSO.

Name of Publication

Regulations and Guidance

Volume 1	Court Orders
Volume 2	Family Support, Day Care and Educational Provision for Young Children
Volume 3	Family Placements
Volume 4	Residential Care
Volume 5	Independent Schools
Volume 6	Children with Disabilities
Volume 7	Guardians ad Litem (GALs) and Court Procedures
Volume 8	Private Fostering and Miscellaneous
Volume 9	Adoption Issues

foreword

The Children Act which received Royal Assent on 16 November 1989 is the most comprehensive piece of legislation which Parliament has ever enacted about children. It draws together and simplifies existing legislation to produce a more practical and consistent code. It integrates the law relating to private individuals with the responsibilities of public authorities, in particular local authority social services departments, towards children. In so doing the Act strikes a new balance between family autonomy and the protection of children.

It is intended that, apart from the small number of provisions which come into force on Royal Assent or shortly after, the Act will be implemented as a whole in October 1991. *This document treats the Act as if it were in force now and refers in the past tense to the legislation which is repealed by the Act.*

This introductory guide is necessarily confined to the substantive provisions of the Act itself. Under it, regulations and rules of court will be prepared in advance of implementation and details notified separately. Generally, the Act applies only to England and Wales. The most important exception is that Part X (Child Minding and Day Care for Young Children) applies also in Scotland. A number of consequential amendments are also made to the law in Scotland and Northern Ireland. Section 90 lists the provisions which apply to those countries.

The Government has started a review of the law relating to adoption in England and Wales. In Scotland a major review of child care legislation is under way. Other aspects of family law are under consideration by the Law Commission. Further proposals for reform of family law and jurisdiction can therefore be expected in due course. For England and Wales these initiatives are part of a structured programme which will build on the framework established by the Children Act.

The intention of this document is not to provide a substitute for the Children Act itself. That Act has been drafted in a clear style which should make it accessible to non-lawyers. However, the Act does cover a large amount of ground and it is hoped that this Introduction will help the reader to steer a safe path, to understand the Act as a whole and not to lose sight of underlying principles. The Government is not entitled to give an authoritative interpretation of the law and ultimately any interpretation of the Act is a matter for the courts.

Department of Health
Lord Chancellor's Department
Home Office
Department of Education and Science
Scottish Office
Welsh Office

November 1989

The Departments acknowledge with gratitude the help of Jonathan Whybrow for the preparation of this Introduction. He worked on the Children Bill Team and is now of John Howell and Co. (Solicitors), Sheffield.

NOTE ON TERMINOLOGY

Throughout the Act, the words 'parent' and 'relative' include the parents and relatives of any child, whether or not his parents are or have been married to each other.

With the exception of some of the financial provisions in Schedule 1 of the Act, a 'child' means a person who has not reached eighteen years of age.

Throughout, references are usually made to 'he', 'his' or 'him', although in the Act nothing turns on the sex of the person referred to and the references equally could be to 'she', 'hers' or 'her'.

The following terms have particular meanings which it may be easy to overlook:

(a) 'a relative' of a child means a grandparent, brother, sister, uncle or aunt (whether of the full blood or half blood or by affinity) or step-parent;

(b) where a child is said to be in local authority 'care', he is under a care order. 'Care' no longer indicates a child who is accommodated by a local authority on a voluntary basis. In the Children Act children who are accommodated by or on behalf of a local authority are referred to as 'looked after' by a local authority, whether the accommodation is provided voluntarily or compulsorily. Where a person is described as having 'care' of the child in a non-technical sense, the word 'care' has its ordinary meaning;

(c) 'a supervision order' means a supervision order made under the Act. It does not mean a supervision order made under section 7(7)(b) of the Children and Young Persons Act 1969 (in respect of a juvenile offender) nor does it indicate an education supervision order.

The same terminology is used throughout this Introduction. All references external to this document are in square brackets. All references to this document itself are in round brackets.

contents

4. LOCAL AUTHORITY SERVICES FOR CHILDREN AND FAMILIES — 44

5. CHILDREN WHO ARE LOOKED AFTER BY LOCAL AUTHORITIES — 50

6. THE PROTECTION OF CHILDREN AT RISK — 60

7. THE WELFARE OF CHILDREN AWAY FROM HOME — 74

8.   ADOPTION, EVIDENCE, PROCEDURE AND OTHER MATTERS   85

CHAPTER 1 INTRODUCTION

1.1 The law about caring for, bringing up and protecting children was inconsistent and fragmented across the face of the statute book. The Children Act brings about radical changes and improvements in the law and provides a single and consistent statement of it.

1.2 The decisions of the courts about children and the powers and duties of local authorities give wide scope for discretion. It is important to grasp the broad objectives which the legislation aims to achieve and the tools which it employs. The Act gives the opportunity to rethink practices and unless this is done there will be lost a rare and vital opportunity to improve the lot of children. The purpose of the following paragraphs is to highlight the major elements of the Act and to explain how they can contribute to improving the care, upbringing and protection of children.

CHILDREN IN THEIR FAMILIES

1.3 The Act rests on the belief that children are generally best looked after within the family with both parents playing a full part and without resort to legal proceedings. That belief is reflected in:
- the new concept of parental responsibility;
- the ability of unmarried fathers to share that responsibility by agreement with the mother;
- the local authorities' duty to give support for children and their families;
- the local authorities' duty to return a child looked after by them to his family unless this is against his interests;
- the local authorities' duty to ensure contact with his parents whenever possible for a child looked after by them away from home.

Parental Responsibility

1.4 The Act uses the phrase '*parental responsibility*' to sum up the collection of duties, rights and authority which a parent has in respect of his child. That choice of words emphasises that the duty to care for the child and to raise him to moral, physical and emotional health is the fundamental task of parenthood and the only justification for the authority it confers.

1.5 The importance of parental responsibility is emphasised in the Act by the fact that not only is it unaffected by the separation of parents but even when courts make orders in private proceedings such as divorce, that responsibility continues and is limited only to the extent that any order settles certain concrete issues between the parties. That arrangement aims to emphasise that interventions by the courts where there is family breakdown should not be regarded as lessening the duty on both parents to continue to play a full part in the child's upbringing.

1.6 The Act makes it easier for unmarried fathers to obtain parental responsibility. The aim as with other provisions in the Act is to encourage both parents to participate in the child's upbringing. Previously, an unmarried father who wanted to share parental responsibility with the mother had to obtain a court order. Under the Act, if both parents are content it can be done by a simple agreement and without going to court.

Support for Children and Families

1.7 Local authorities have a new duty to promote the upbringing of children in need by their families so far as is consistent with their welfare. 'Children in need' covers children who need services to secure a reasonable standard of health and development and includes children who are disabled. This broad duty which comprehends and extends the present duty to reduce the need for children to be in care or brought before the courts is a key provision and is elaborated in the range of services to be provided as set out in Schedule 2 of the Act.

1.8 One particular service in this part of the Act is given prominence because of its importance for family support — day care and supervised activities for pre-school children, and school aged children outside school hours and in the holidays. Here the local authority have a duty to provide for children in need and a power to provide more generally, with help by way of training and advice to those caring for the children. Because of the need to coordinate what is provided with nursery school provision and to let the local community know what the situation is, the Act expects social services departments with the education departments to publish a review of this provision every three years.

CHILDREN AWAY FROM HOME

Children Looked After By Local Authorities

1.9 The Act begins from the standpoint that when a local authority has to arrange for a child to live away from home, for a shorter or a longer period, because the parents are unable to care for him properly or need respite. This should preferably be under voluntary arrangements with the parents who will retain their parental responsibility acting so far as possible as partners of the local authority and the substitute carers. They should participate in the child's care and retain contact, so that the child can return as soon as it is in his interest to do so.

1.10 Administrative measures to exercise compulsion when the child is looked after, whether to limit contact or to prevent the parent recovering the child, are abolished by the Act which provides for a range of court orders for those situations when the child needs protection from his parents, or a secure substitute family.

1.11 Even when the child is under a care order the Act provides for the parents to retain parental responsibility (although the local authority may limit its operation), to be involved in local authority decision making and for them to have reasonable contact with the child unless the court provides otherwise.

1.12 The Act contains a modern formulation of the welfare duty which governs local authorities' decisions in relation to a child looked after by them, in particular the child's racial origin and cultural and linguistic background are recognised as important factors to be taken into account. There is a new requirement to prepare a child for leaving the local authority's responsibility and for continuing to advise and assist him after leaving up to the age of 21.

1.13 The Act assumes that local authorities will plan their services for children whom they are looking after and provides for regulations to require them to review their provision at intervals. It also requires them to have a complaints procedure with an independent element. This part of the Act builds on current thinking on best practice which emphasizes the desirability of involving parents and children in the services provided for them.

Other Children Looked After Away from Home.

1.14 The Act rationalises and extends the legal framework for safeguarding the welfare of children living away from home in institutions such as private and voluntary homes, independent and maintained schools, private and NHS hospitals. Broadly speaking it does this by giving the proprietor of the non-state facilities a duty towards the child and the local authority a responsibility, adjusted to the type of institution where the child is, to take appropriate steps to check that the duty is complied with or that the child's welfare is safeguarded.

1.15 Similarly the local authority's responsibilities to young children (under eight) in private and voluntary day care have been reviewed and re-enacted in an improved form. The purpose is to give parents some reassurance that basic standards are reached in the private and voluntary sector in the interests of protection of the child. The local authority's powers and duties in respect of private fostering have been simplified and improved to provide a more effective framework for the protection of children who are placed with private foster parents.

ONLY POSITIVE INTERVENTION

1.16 The Act prohibits a court from making any order unless it is satisfied that the order will positively contribute to the child's welfare.

1.17 This has two aims. The first is to discourage court orders being made in all private proceedings such as divorce simply as part of a package. If orders are restricted to where they address a demonstrable need this should reduce conflict and promote parental agreement and co-operation.

1.18 The second aim is to ensure that the court, when considering whether to make a care or supervision order, will consider whether the order will positively improve the child's welfare. In the past there has been some concern that once the grounds for making such an order are made out, orders are made irrespective of whether that will benefit the child or be bad for him.

LESS DELAY

1.19 The Act makes it clear that delay in court proceedings is generally harmful to children and should be avoided. The court is expected to draw up a timetable and take appropriate measures to reduce delay to a minimum.

GETTING THE BEST FOR CHILDREN

The Child's Welfare is Paramount

1.20 The overriding purpose of the Act is to promote and safeguard the welfare of children. That purpose is seen at its clearest in the opening provision of the Act. It tells all courts to treat the welfare of the child as the paramount consideration when reaching any decision about his upbringing (or, incidentally, the administration or application of his property). The word 'paramount' repeats the previous legislation. It emphasises that no change is intended from the current position. Thus, whilst the courts are to take into account all the relevant surrounding circumstances, including, for example, the wishes of parents, at the end of the day they must do what is best for the child.

A Checklist

1.21 The Act greatly increases the court's ability to do what is best for the child. To begin with it contains a checklist of matters which are to be considered in most court hearings about whether to make an order and which order to make, focusing particularly on the needs of the child but also on his own views and on the options available to the court.

Greater Choice

1.22 The checklist makes it clear that the court is to have regard to all the orders available when reaching a decision. Thus, whatever the order applied for in private proceedings, the court may make any other private order if it thinks it is best for the child or may trigger a local authority investigation to see whether the authority should apply for one of the orders available to protect the child. The court can also exercise all these powers of its own motion in any appropriate family proceedings, whether or not they are specifically about the child.

1.23 That full menu of orders is also available to a court hearing a local authority application for a care or other order in respect of a child. Thus a court might, for example, order that a child live with a suitable relative or friend rather than make a care order in favour of a local authority. Or it may mix and match by, for example, ordering that the child live with a non-abusing parent and making a supervision order at the same time.

THE CHILD AND HIS VIEWS IN PROCEEDINGS

1.24 The checklist of particular matters to which the court is to have regard in reaching decisions about the child is headed by the child's wishes and feelings and highlights the great importance attached to them.

In Private Proceedings

1.25 The Act in the area of private law seeks to strike a balance between the need to recognise the child as an independent person and to ensure that his views are fully taken into account, and the risk of casting on him the burden of resolving problems caused by his parents or requiring him to choose between them. As well as including his views in the checklist, the Act allows the child with the court's permission to seek an order about his own future. The child will also be able to be joined as a party if the court thinks fit even if he does not seek an order.

1.26 Whether or not the child is a party to proceedings, the court has the power to commission a welfare report and to ensure that it covers his wishes and feelings.

In Local Authority Proceedings

1.27 In local authority proceedings, for example an application for a care order, the child is always to be a party. Generally the court will also appoint a trained social worker as his guardian *ad litem*. It will then be the guardian's duty to represent the child in these proceedings and safeguard the child's interests. The child will be entitled to separate legal representation and if the child and the guardian do not agree about the case, the solicitor will take his instructions from the child rather than the guardian.

1.28 In private law proceedings between parents or other individuals, the orders available under the Act look to practicalities rather than legal rights. Thus the courts have the power to make orders about:

- with whom the child will live (residence orders);
- any form of contact he is to have with other people (contact orders);
- any other particular matter concerning the child and upbringing (specific issue orders), or,
- to prohibit anything being done in relation to the child (prohibited steps orders).

1.29 Unlike custody orders, they will not remove parental power and authority from one parent or confer sole power and authority on the other. Rather they will simply settle particular matters which neither party may then upset. Parents will still be able to act as parents in ways which are not affected by the order. The orders themselves are much more flexible, allowing the court to make whatever arrangements seem best in the particular case, but dealing with practical questions rather than abstract rights. Wardship remains available to private individuals but the new orders should make the need to use it rarer.

1.30 In addition, the Act enables courts to make short term family assistance orders which require a welfare officer to advise, assist and befriend members of a family. Their major purpose is to provide help to the family in the immediate aftermath of family breakdown, in particular where they are difficulties about matters such as contact between children and an estranged parent.

PROTECTION OF CHILDREN

The Welfare Balance

1.31 The Act seeks to protect children both from the harm which can arise from failures or abuse within the family and from the harm which can be caused by unwarranted intervention in their family life. There is a tension between those objectives which the Act seeks to regulate so as to optimise the overall protection provided for children in general. It does this in a number of ways.

Protective Orders

1.32 The courts are given wide powers to intervene to protect children at risk of harm within the family. Provided that the preconditions are established the courts have discretion to:

- order the assessment of a child where there is a real suspicion of harm;
- order the removal or the retention of a child in an emergency;
- order that a child be put under local authority care or supervision pending a full investigation and hearing of the proceedings;
- order that a child be put under the longer term care or supervision of a local authority;
- make private law orders altering the arrangements about with whom the child lives, regulating his contact with other people; determining any particular matter relating to his upbringing and prohibiting any particular step being taken in respect of him.

Protection from 'Protection'

1.33 These necessarily potent powers, if misdirected, may themselves cause harm to a child by enabling the state to intervene in his or his family's life when it should not. Accordingly, the Act seeks to target the powers on cases where the circumstances are such that on balance the bringing of proceedings is likely to be in the best interest of children. It must be remembered, however, that the fact that the preconditions for an order are satisfied is not a reason for making it. Rather it merely brings the case within the target area. An order should only be made if the court is also satisfied that the order it is considering will:
- positively contribute to the child's well being, and
- be in his best interests.

The preconditions which must be satisfied are as set out in paragraphs 1.34 to 1.46 below.

Care and Supervision Orders

1.34 The preconditions are that the child is suffering or is likely to suffer significant harm because of a lack of reasonable parental care or because he is beyond parental control. Reasonable parental care is that care which a **reasonable parent** would provide for the child concerned. Thus a standard of care which would be reasonable for a normal healthy child may not be reasonable if the child has special needs because, say, he has brittle bones, or is asthmatic or mentally disabled.

1.35 The fact that particular parents suffer from limitations such as low intelligence or physical disablement is not relevant to whether the care they are providing is reasonable. What is expected is the care which the average or reasonable parent would provide for that child. It follows that if a parent cannot cope with a child because of personal difficulties, he or she will be acting unreasonably if help is not sought, such as local authority services, including accommodation for the child.

1.36 The preconditions could also cover cases where the child is being looked after and his parent wishes to take him back. For example, in a rare case a parent might fall below the standard of reasonable parental care by insisting on the return of a child from foster parents if the disturbance caused would harm the child to such an extent that it outweighs the benefits of being brought up by his own parent.

Interim Care and Supervision Orders

1.37 The preconditions are the same as for a final order except instead of being satisfied on a balance of probabilities that the preconditions are satisfied, the court has only to conclude that there is reasonable grounds for believing that the circumstances are as described in the preconditions.

Emergency Protection Orders

1.38 The preconditions are that there is reasonable cause to believe that the child is likely to suffer significant harm unless:
- he is removed from where he is to another place, or
- he is kept where he is.

Alternatively, if during the course of an investigation, the enquiries are frustrated by the parents' unreasonable withholding of access to the child and there is reasonable cause to believe that access is required as a matter of urgency, the precondition is satisfied.

1.39 These preconditions are based on the premise that the order can only ever be justified if there is sufficient evidence to indicate a risk of significant harm. It is not, for example, justified simply to enable a local authority or someone on their behalf to investigate a case of suspected abuse.

Child Assessment Order

1.40 If an assessment of the child is needed to decide whether significant harm is likely and it is clear that there is not an emergency calling for an emergency protection order, the Act allows an application for an order for an assessment which can last up to seven days. The order will only be available where notice of the application is given to those involved and after a full hearing in which all sides can be represented and heard.

1.41 This is a different sort of order in that it does not convey parental responsibility to the holder and the court directs what the assessment should be. The order is likely to be useful when the parents or carers are uncooperative and there is concern that the child's needs are not being met but an application for an interim care or supervision order is not appropriate. While seven days may well not be sufficient to complete a multi-disciplinary assessment of the child it should be adequate for a decision to be reached as to what further action, if any, is required.

Private Law Orders

1.42 The court may use private law orders to protect children as well as to resolve disputes between parents. Generally they are available as an alternative to the 'public law' orders listed above or on the application of anyone who has or can show a proper interest in the child. To protect against these orders being used improperly to interfere in families, those who can apply for an order are generally limited to parents and others who have some legal responsibility for the child or who have cared for him for a substantial period. But other people will be able to apply if they get the court's permission (although there are special rules about local authority foster parents, who are in a rather different position from members of the child's family).

The Inherent Jurisdiction

1.43 Local authorities will no longer be able to use the general power of the High Court to act for the good of children (usually through wardship proceedings) as an alternative to care or supervision orders or otherwise to obtain compulsory powers over the child. However, if the High Court is persuaded that there is a likelihood of significant harm to a child if these powers are not invoked and that the matter is one for which the Act makes no provision the High Court may use its inherent powers to intervene. The purpose of this provision is to provide a safety net to cover circumstances not envisaged by the Act.

Limitations on Orders

1.44 In addition to preconditions which aim to limit applications for orders to a general 'target area' the effects of orders are tailored to ensure on the one hand that they confer sufficient power to safeguard and promote the child's interests, and on the other that they restrict those powers so as to avoid an unnecessary degree of interference, and to give the parents a proper opportunity to challenge them.

1.45 Thus, for example, emergency protection orders last for only a maximum of eight days initially and can be extended only up to a maximum of 15 days (and if obtained without the parents being present are challengeable after 72 hours). The holder of an emergency order should only remove the child from home if necessary to safeguard his welfare and is under a duty to return or allow the child to return home if it appears that there is no risk to him. Both interim orders and the emergency orders can contain court directions on the assessment of the child.

1.46 The child assessment order is limited to a maximum of seven days during which the child may only be kept away from home as directed by the court as necessary for the assessment. Interim orders are time limited with a maximum of eight weeks initially and extendable by the court by four weeks at a time beyond that limit.

MOBILISING THE COURTS

Making the Best Use of Judicial Resources

1.47 Cases under the Act may be heard by a magistrates' or county court or the High Court but rules will be made allocating at least some types of cases between the courts and allowing for them to be transferred. In particular, local authority proceedings involving the protection of children will start in a magistrates' court but will be transferable to a county court or the High Court where their weight or complexity justifies it. It is also intended to provide for transfer between courts to avoid unnecessary delay or to allow cases involving the same child and his family to be heard together. Most private family cases will be heard along with other proceedings about the same family (such as divorce) as they were under the old law. Details of which cases will be transferable and in what circumstances are still to be decided (as at November 1989).

1.48 The procedures of the courts are being reviewed. One aim is to make sure that the procedures in different courts are as uniform as possible or at least compatible.

1.49 The result for magistrates is likely to mean much more disclosure of the parties' evidence and cases ahead of the hearing, greater reliance on written material and magistrates reading the papers before the hearing and giving reasons for their decision at the end. Specially trained magistrates will sit as a 'family proceedings court' with power to hear care-related cases as well as all other magistrates' family and children's cases.

1.50 In the county courts and the High Court it is hoped to concentrate the work in the hands of a limited number of specialists who will have made a particular study of children's matters.

A More Active Court

1.51 Under the Act the courts have an independent duty to do what is best for the child. If the courts are to discharge that duty often they will have to take an active part in the proceedings rather than simply acting as umpires between the contending parties.

1.52 Greater disclosure of evidence ahead of the hearing is meant to encourage courts to take a more active role in the proceedings. The power in the Act to allow courts to draw up timetables and give directions to ensure that they are adhered to requires more active involvement by the courts. And courts are encouraged to make use of the guardian *ad litem* in local authority cases to ensure that the case and the options for action are fully explored.

CHAPTER 2   PARENTAL RESPONSIBILITY

2.1 The law gives a collection of rights, powers, duties and responsibilities to parents. In the Act these are referred to collectively as 'parental responsibility'. Under the old law, the rules which governed who may acquire parental responsibility and when it could be exercised were unclear, particularly if a child was subject to a custody order. Only in certain matters, such as the right to withhold agreement to a child's adoption or the right to inherit property when a child dies, has the law been specific.

2.2 The courts have come to regard parental responsibility as a collection of powers and duties which follow from being a parent and bringing up a child, rather than as rights which may be enforced at law. The exercise of parental responsibility is left largely to the discretion of the adults involved, subject to two limitations. First, the criminal law imposes minimum standards of care and civil law provides remedies for the protection of children's welfare [*the Children and Young Persons Acts 1933–1969 and the Child Care Act 1980] (for the changes to the civil law, see particularly Chapters 3 and 6)*. Secondly, parental responsibility itself diminishes as the child acquires sufficient understanding to make his own decisions [*Gillick v. West Norfolk and Wisbech Area Health Authority [1986] A.C. 112*]. It would not be realistic or desirable to attempt to prescribe in statute the content of parental responsibility. However, the Act does put on a consistent basis rules about who acquires parental responsibility, when it may be exercised and what effect an order under the Act will have upon this.

2.3 'Parental responsibility' is defined to include all the rights, powers, authority and duties of parents in relation to a child and his property [*section 3(1)*]. The value of the term parental responsibility is twofold. First, it unifies the many references in legislation to parental rights, powers and the rest. Secondly, it more accurately reflects that the true nature of most parental rights is of limited powers to carry out parental duties.

2.4 The effect of having parental responsibility is to empower a person to take most decisions in the child's life (subject to the limitations mentioned above). It does not make him a parent or relative of the child in law, for example to give him rights of inheritance, or to place him under a statutory duty to maintain a child [*section 3(4)*].

WHO HAS PARENTAL RESPONSIBILITY?

2.5 Where a child's parents were or have been married to each other at or after the time of his conception, they each have parental responsibility for him [*section 2(1), as extended by section 1 of the Family Law Reform Act 1987: section 2(3)*]. Otherwise, the mother alone has parental responsibility unless the father acquires it by a court order or an agreement under the Act [*section 2(2)*].

2.6 The father who does not have parental responsibility may acquire it in one of two ways:

(a) with the mother, he may make 'a parental responsibility agreement'; or

(b) he may apply to court for an order which gives him parental responsibility [*section 4(1)*].

2.7 A parental responsibility agreement was not available under the old law [*although a parent could make an agreement about the exercise of her parental rights and duties under section 1(2) of the Guardianship Act 1973*]. It is intended as a simple and cheap method by which unmarried parents may share parental responsibility without going to court. The agreement must be made in the form prescribed by regulations and, if further regulations are made, will have to be officially recorded in the prescribed manner [*section 4(2)*]. The effect of a parental responsibility agreement is the same as a court order conferring parental responsibility. Both may only be brought to an end by a court order on the application of a person with parental responsibility for the child or (with the leave of the court) of the child himself, if he has sufficient understanding to make the application [*section 4(3) and (4)*].

2.8 A court order which gives a father parental responsibility is similar to an order which gave him parental rights and duties under section 4 of the Family Law Reform Act 1987. [*An order under the 1987 Act which was in force at the commencement of the Children Act is deemed to be an order under section 4 of the latter statute: Schedule 14, paragraph 4*]. An order under section 4 of the Children Act *must* be made if a residence order is made in favour of a father [*section 12(1)*]. *(For residence orders, see paragraph 3.32)*. This is to ensure that a father who is entitled to have the child live with him under a court order will always have parental responsibility for him. If that residence order is later discharged, the parental responsibility order will not come to an end unless the court specifically decides that it should [*section 12(4)*]. *(For the position where an unmarried father has an order under the old law giving him care and control or custody of the child, see paragraph 3.128)*.

WHO ELSE MAY ACQUIRE PARENTAL RESPONSIBILITY?

2.9 People other than parents may acquire parental responsibility by the private appointment of a guardian or an order of the court (a residence order, a care order, an emergency protection order or an order appointing a guardian).

Guardianship

2.10 A guardian may be appointed to take over parental responsibility for a child when a parent with parental responsibility dies. A guardian may be any other individual (including a parent). A local authority or voluntary organisation cannot be a guardian, since they are not 'individuals'. He acquires parental responsibility (if he does not already have it) when the appointment takes effect and may appoint another guardian to act if he should die while the child is still under eighteen [*section 5(3), (4) and (6)*]. Guardians also acquire the right to agree (or to withhold agreement) to the child's adoption [*Adoption Act 1976, section 16*]. The Act clarifies the law of guardianship, enables appointments to be made more simply and introduces a number of new provisions which recognise that guardians are generally intended to take over the care of a child where he would not otherwise have a parent with parental responsibility.

2.11 Private appointments may be made by a parent who has parental responsibility for the child or a person who has already been appointed guardian [*section 5(3) and (4)*]. An appointment must be in writing, dated and signed by (or at the direction of) the maker [*section 5(5)*]. If it is made at the appointer's direction, the making must be attested by two witnesses. An appointment may be made in a will or by deed, as under the old law, but does not have to be made in these ways.

2.12 Private appointments will no longer always come into effect on the death of the maker. If, on the maker's death, the child still has a parent with parental responsibility, the appointment will not take effect until that parent also dies [*section 5(7) and (8)*]. The exception to this rule is that if, on the maker's death, there was a residence order in his favour, the appointment takes effect immediately (unless the residence order was also in favour of a surviving parent of the child) [*section 5(7) and (9)*]. Where a residence order was not in existence in favour of the appointing parent (or there was a joint residence order in favour of the appointer and a surviving parent), it is presumed that the surviving parent ought to be left to care for the child as he wishes. If he wants to seek the help or advice of the 'guardian' he may always do so. On his death, however, the guardian's appointment takes effect.

2.13 Private appointments may be made individually or by people acting together [*section 5(10)*]. More than one guardian may be appointed by the same person or persons. A later appointment of a guardian (which is not clearly additional) will revoke an earlier one by the same person [*section 6(1)*]. A private appointment may also be revoked, either in writing which is dated and signed by the maker (or at his direction) [*section 6(2)*]. If the revocation is signed at the maker's direction, the signature must be in his presence and that of two witnesses who attest or by destruction of the appointment by the maker (or in his presence and at his direction) with the intention of revocation [*section 6(3)*]. An appointment made in a will or a codicil is revoked if the will or codicil is revoked [*section 6(4)*].

2.14 The guardian may disclaim his appointment in signed writing provided that he acts within a reasonable time of learning that the appointment has taken effect [*section 6(5)*]. Regulations may be made prescribing the manner of recording disclaimers [*section 6(6)*]. He may also be discharged by a court order made on the application of any person who has parental responsibility for the child, the child (if he has sufficient understanding) or by the court of its own initiative in family proceedings [*section 6(7)*]. (*For family proceedings, see paragraphs 3.5–3.7*).

2.15 A court may appoint a guardian in similar circumstances to those in which a private appointment may take effect, namely:
(a) where a child has no parent with parental responsibility for him; or
(b) where, even though he still has such a parent, his other parent or a guardian of his has died and, immediately before his death, the deceased had a residence order in his favour in respect of the child [*section 5(1)*].

2.16 No court appointment may be made under 2.15(b) if the residence order in question was also in favour of a surviving parent of the child [*section 5(9)*]. Court appointments may be made on the application of the person who would like to be guardian or by the court of its own initiative in family proceedings [*section 5(1) and (2)*].

2.17 Guardians appointed by the court may be discharged in the same circumstances as private appointments.

Residence Orders

2.18 A residence order may be made under Part II of the Act in order to settle the arrangements as to the person with whom a child is to live (*paragraphs 3.32 et seq*). If such an order is made in favour of a person who is not a parent or guardian of the child, it gives parental responsibility to him [*section 12(2)*].

2.19 A person who acquires parental responsibility under a residence order (i.e. someone who is not a parent or a guardian) does not acquire the right to agree or refuse to agree to the child's adoption (or other related adoption orders) or to appoint a guardian of the child [*section 12(3)*].

Care and Emergency Protection Orders

2.20 A residence order may not be made in favour of a local authority [*section 9(2)*]. However, a care order places a child in the care of a local authority, which enables them to decide with whom the child will live, and also gives them parental responsibility [*section 33(1) and (3)(a)*]. It does not give them the right to agree or refuse to agree to adoption or to appoint a guardian [*section 33(6)(b)*]. It also does not enable them to cause the child to be brought up in a religious persuasion other than the one in which he would have been brought up if the order had not been made [*section 33(6)(a)*].

2.21 Emergency protection orders are short term orders which entitle the applicant to remove the child from (or to prevent him from being removed to) a situation of apprehended danger (*Chapter 6*). These orders confer parental responsibility on the applicant for the period of the order [*section 44(4)(c)*]. A person with parental responsibility under an emergency protection order must take (but may only take) action which is reasonably required to safeguard or promote the child's welfare (bearing in mind the duration of the order) [*section 44(5)(b)*].

THE EXERCISE OF PARENTAL RESPONSIBILITY

2.22 The fact that one person acquires parental responsibility does not in itself remove another's parental responsibility [*section 2(6)*]. After separation or divorce parents retain their parental responsibility. However, a person who has parental responsibility is not entitled to act incompatibly with a court order [*section 2(8)*]. (*As regards orders made under the old law, see the transitional provisions referred to in paragraphs 3.127 and 3.128*). In exceptional circumstances, he may be required to disobey an order which would otherwise put the child at risk. [*Pursuant to the duty not to cause unnecessary suffering in section 1 of the Children and Young Persons Act 1933*].

2.23 Parental responsibility for a child cannot be passed on to someone else or otherwise be given up [*section 2(9)*]. However, where he acquired parental responsibility under a court order (or parental responsibility agreement or private appointment of a guardian), the court may later bring that order (or agreement or appointment) to an end.

2.24 A person with parental responsibility may arrange for another person to meet that responsibility on his behalf [*section 2(9)*]. Such an arrangement might be useful while a person with parental responsibility is unable to act, perhaps due to a stay in hospital or a trip abroad. It does not affect any liability of the person with parental responsibility which follows from a failure to meet his parental responsibility [*section 2(11)*].

2.25 Where more than one person has parental responsibility for a child at the same time, one may act independently of the other or others to meet that responsibility [*section 2(5) and (7)*]. The Act does not repeat the old law in its attempts to impose a duty on one parent to consult the other or to give one a right of veto against the action of the other. If necessary, one person with parental responsibility may ask a court to make an order which would require another person to inform him before a particular step is taken or not taken [*Such an order may be made under Part II of the Act*] (*see paragraph 3.32*). The onus of applying to court should not generally fall on the person who is caring for the child. This person (who will usually be the child's mother) needs to be able to respond to circumstances as they arise in order to meet her parental responsibility.

2.26 The only exception to the rule which permits independent action to meet shared parental responsibility arises when a child is in care. Here, the local authority is given power to determine the extent to which another person with parental responsibility may act. (*This is explained in paragraphs 5.4 and 5.5*).

CARE BUT NOT PARENTAL RESPONSIBILITY

2.27 If a person has care of a child for whom he does not have parental responsibility, section 3(5) of the Act empowers him to do what is reasonable in all the circumstances to safeguard or promote the child's welfare. This is the person who in old terminology had 'actual custody' of the child. Of course, such a person may not act in a way which conflicts with the Act, in particular with an order under it, except in the limited circumstances in which he may be required to protect the child from danger.

TRANSITIONAL PROVISIONS

2.28 Where a guardian's appointment took effect before implementation of the Act, he is treated as if he had been appointed under the Act [*Schedule 14, paragraph 12(1)*]. He therefore acquires parental responsibility for the child concerned. However, any appointment which has not taken effect by that date will only have effect in accordance with the Act [*Schedule 14, paragraph 13*], so that the rules which limit the circumstances in which appointments have effect apply.

CHAPTER 3 COURT PROCEEDINGS

3.1 The old public and private law relating to children was unnecessarily complicated. The procedures and remedies overlapped and produced many anomalies. The result was that the law seemed to lack guiding principles and was unintelligible to many of those involved, either as participants or practitioners [*for details, see Law Commission Report No. 172: Guardianship and Custody (1988)*].

3.2 The Children Act was drafted with these criticisms in mind. The aim was to produce a single and consistent scheme which would be flexible enough to meet whatever circumstances may arise. Throughout, however, there has been a need to strike the right balance between two principles. The first is that parents generally ought to be able to bring up their children as they consider best and, where appropriate, with state support. The second is that the state must have adequate power to protect children at risk, if necessary by removing them from their home. When it comes to children, legislation can only set out basic ground rules. The Children Act is intended to establish a framework to enable fair and reasonable decisions to be made.

3.3 The Act abolishes custody and access orders (and their offshoots), unifies the many routes by which a child may be placed in the care of a local authority or under supervision and replaces the jurisdiction to make orders under fifteen statutes. Supervision orders may still be made in criminal proceedings under the Children and Young Persons Act 1969. The Act replaces order-making powers in the Custody of Children Act 1891, Children and Young Persons Acts 1933–1969, Nurseries and Child Minders Regulation Act 1948, Sexual Offences Act 1956, Family Law Reform Act 1969, Guardianship Acts 1971–73, Matrimonial Causes Act 1973, Children Act 1975, Domestic Proceedings and Magistrates' Courts Act 1978, Child Care Act 1980, Foster Children Act 1980, Children's Homes Act 1982 and Family Law Reform Act 1987. It also removes some order making powers under the Adoption Act 1976.

3.4 The Children Act creates a single code for court orders about the welfare of children. The main features of this code are that for the first time:

(a) each court which is considering a matter affecting a child's future will be able to make orders in the interests of the child's welfare;

(b) any person will be able to apply to court for an order concerning a child's upbringing (either with or without the court's leave);

(c) the range of orders available in each court and the criteria applied by the courts will be the same;

(d) the effect of court orders is clarified, including the effect of one order on another;

(e) where aspects of a case affecting the same child come before more than one court, the proceedings can be brought together in one venue.

3.5 This Chapter is a guide to all court proceedings under the Act about children except those for emergency protection, child assessment and recovery orders under Part V, which are dealt with in Chapter 6. Applications can be made principally under Parts I, II and IV of the Act and proceedings under these Parts are classed as 'family proceedings' [*section 8(3) and (4)*]. This term is important for two reasons. First, the court has full order-making powers in such proceedings and, secondly, the rules which permit separate proceedings to be consolidated come into play. 'Family proceedings' are the key to the Act's flexibility.

3.6 Certain other proceedings come within the definition of family proceedings so that the same flexibility is extended to them [*section 8(3) and (4)*]. These proceedings are in connection with:

(a) adoption [*Adoption Act 1976*];

(b) the exercise of the inherent jurisdiction of the High Court in relation to children (usually wardship). This jurisdiction is 'inherent' in that it does not derive from statute;

(c) divorce, judicial separation and nullity of marriage [*Matrimonial Causes Act 1973 and Part III of the Matrimonial and Family Proceedings Act 1984*];

(d) applications for financial relief between spouses [*The 1973 Act and the Domestic Proceedings and Magistrates' Courts Act 1978*]; and

(e) domestic violence and occupation of the matrimonial home [*Domestic Violence and Matrimonial Proceedings Act 1976, the 1978 Act and sections 1 and 9 of the Matrimonial Homes Act 1983*].

3.7 In these proceedings the court has full power to make orders in respect of children. This is similar to the position under the old law in divorce and other proceedings listed in (c) and (d) above, although the range of orders which may be made has increased. However, in domestic violence cases the court used to have no power to make orders about the care of the children. In adoption proceedings the court had only limited power to make custody, care and supervision orders. The wardship court had developed its own range of orders, which were generally outside the statutory scheme; now it *also* has full powers under the Act. (*The effect of the Act on wardship is considered further in paragraphs 3.118–3.123*).

3.8 With a few limited exceptions [*for example, financial orders under Schedule 1, see paragraph 1(1)*], orders under the Act may be made in the High Court, county courts or magistrates' courts: jurisdiction is said to be 'concurrent'. Within magistrates' courts, the power of juvenile courts to make care and other public law orders is transferred to domestic courts with the exception of those supervision orders which are made in criminal proceedings in juvenile courts. In future, domestic courts will hear all family proceedings heard by magistrates. These courts will be renamed 'family proceedings courts' and justices sitting in such courts will be drawn from 'family panels' which will replace existing domestic panels.

3.9 While jurisdiction is generally concurrent, the Lord Chancellor may order that certain proceedings must start in specified courts [*Schedule 11, paragraph 1*]. The exercise of this power is still under consideration; however, it is likely that proceedings under the Act in county and magistrates' courts will have to start in a court which is local to where the child usually lives. An exception to this rule is likely to be that where the child is the subject of family proceedings in one court, proceedings under the Act should also start in that court. The converse could also be achieved: an order may require that any family proceedings which may affect the child should start in a court in which proceedings under the Act are already pending.

3.10 The 'start' rules will be complemented by rules for the transfer of proceedings between courts. The Lord Chancellor may order that proceedings under the Act and other family proceedings which may affect the child (other than proceedings under the inherent jurisdiction of the High Court) should be transferred to specified courts [*Schedule 11, paragraph 2*]. The intention is that by a combination of start and transfer rules cases will be directed to the best possible venue. Guidance will be supplied for the operation of these rules. In proceedings relating to care and supervision orders, decisions about the allocation of cases will be taken having regard to factors such as the complexity of the case, its likely duration, the availability of court time and the number of expert witnesses who may be involved. It is hoped that in this way cases will be matched with the most appropriate level of court. In all proceedings under the Act it should be possible to avoid delays which may otherwise build up in certain courts. In particular, it should be possible to consolidate proceedings which relate to the same child in one court, which should reduce the stress and cost of multiple proceedings.

3.11 The targeting of a case to an appropriate court is particularly important in local authority cases, which under the old law were spread across the courts in an uncoordinated way which produced anomalies. The 'start' rules will require that all applications for care and supervision orders under Part IV should be made to a family proceedings court (i.e. a magistrates' court). This is because most of these cases can be appropriately heard by magistrates who have considerable experience in this area. Applications by local authorities will have to be supported by sufficient information about the case to enable a decision about transfer to be made. Where it is clear that the case should be transferred to a different court (another family proceedings court, a county court or the High Court), and in some cases this will be immediately apparent, an order will be made to that effect. The 'start' rules should not become a cause of delay: if, for example, one party wants the case to be transferred to the county court but the family proceedings court disagrees, that party will be able to go straight to a county court registrar to ask him to transfer the case to the county court himself.

3.12 Appeals from magistrates in family proceedings may be made to the High Court [section 94]. The jurisdiction of the Crown Court to hear appeals in proceedings relating to care and supervision orders is abolished.

THE PRINCIPLES WHICH GUIDE THE COURTS

3.13 Section 1 sets out three principles which guide a court which makes decisions under the Act. The first is that the child's welfare is the paramount consideration when a court determines any question with respect to his upbringing ('the welfare principle'). The second is that the court should not make an order under the Act unless it considers that to do so would be better for the child than making no order at all. The third is that the court should have regard to the general principle that delay in determining a question with respect to the upbringing of a child is likely to prejudice his welfare.

3.14 The welfare principle means that the court's decision will be that which most promotes the child's welfare and is in his best interests [*J v. C.[1970] A.C. 668*]. Section 1(1) of the Act replaces section 1 of the Guardianship of Minors Act 1971. Like its predecessor, section 1(1) applies when a court determines any question with respect to a child's upbringing, the administration of a child's property or the application of any income arising from it. Upbringing includes the care of the child but not his maintenance, so that the welfare principle does not apply to financial orders under Schedule 1 [section 105(1)]. The welfare principle also applies to proceedings outside the Act, such as those under the inherent jurisdiction of the High Court.

3.15 The principle in section 1(1) does not mean that every question which is decided by a court under the Act will simply turn on what is best for the child. In a number of instances certain other conditions must be satisfied before the welfare principle comes into play. For example, the court must be satisfied of the conditions in section 31(2) before a care or supervision order may be made (*Paragraph 3.50*). The Act is quite specific about when these other considerations should come to bear [*sections 10(9), 36(3), 38(2), 43(1) and 44(1)*]. Where they are satisfied, the welfare principle then governs the court's decision about whether an order should be made and if so, which one.

3.16 What is best for a child will depend on a consideration of the facts in each case. With the exceptions of the two other general principles discussed below, the Children Act does not attempt to steer the court to a particular conclusion, such as that it is generally in a child's interests for him to maintain contact with both his parents after separation or divorce. Any such guideline would inevitably detract from the duty of the court in each case to decide what is best for the children concerned. However, section 1(3) of the Act supplies a checklist to assist those who have to interpret the welfare principle and those who may be affected by it. The checklist applies to those proceedings in which guidance would seem to be most helpful, namely:

(a) where the making, variation or discharge of a section 8 order (such as a residence or contact order) is opposed by a party to the proceedings; and

(b) where the court is considering whether to make, vary or discharge an order under Part IV (orders relating to care and supervision) [*section 1(4)*].

3.17 The checklist may also be helpful in other proceedings such as those for a section 8 order which are unopposed or those for an order under Part V, but it would not be appropriate to require the court to apply it in every such case. Where, for example, the parties are agreed about the residence or contact order which is applied for, the demands of the checklist might make a court feel that it should order a welfare report which in most cases would be an unnecessary intrusion into the family's circumstances. In proceedings relating to emergency protection orders there may not be time to apply the checklist thoroughly and, in any case, the court may only have heard evidence from one side.

3.18 The checklist is not exhaustive. It simply lists the factors to which the court must particularly have regard when considering whether to make an order. Most of these factors are not new: they have been drawn together from existing case law. They are as follows:

(a) the ascertainable wishes and feelings of the child concerned (considered in the light of his age and understanding);

(b) his physical, emotional and educational needs;

(c) the likely effect on him of any change in his circumstances;

(d) his age, sex, background and any characteristics of his which the court considers relevant;

(e) any harm which he has suffered or is at risk of suffering;

(f) how capable each of his parents, and any other person in relation to whom the court considers the question to be relevant, is of meeting his needs;

(g) the range of powers available to the court under the Act in the proceedings in question.

3.19 Two factors which may lead to some change in practice are found in (a) and (g) above. The former refers to the ascertainable wishes and feelings of the child concerned in the proceedings, which are to be considered in the light of his age and understanding. It is sometimes said that the courts have paid insufficient regard to the child's perspective and paragraph (a) is intended to remedy this. There is a similar requirement in adoption legislation. The child's wishes and feelings will usually be ascertained and presented to the court by a welfare officer or guardian *ad litem*. It is not intended that an unwilling child should be placed in the position of having to decide between the claims of competing adults or that a child will usually be legally represented in most family proceedings (*paragraph 3.117*). Rather, (a) underlines the duty of those involved of their duty to take account of the child's wishes and feelings.

3.20 In the checklist above, (g) requires the court to consider its range of powers in the proceedings in question. This factor reflects how the Children Act opens up the courts' order-making powers. As will be explained below (*paragraph 3.30*), in any family proceedings the court may make any order under the Act (provided that, in some cases, specific conditions are fulfilled and an application has been made). In contrast, the jurisdiction to make orders under the old law depended on the statute under which the proceedings were taken. The checklist, therefore, requires the court to consider all the options which are available to it.

The Presumption of No Order

3.21 Section 1(5) introduces a new principle which prevents an order being made under the Act unless the court considers that making it would be better for the child than making no order at all. It creates a presumption against a court order being made: no order may be made unless it can be shown to be beneficial to the child.

3.22 Section 1(5) addresses two features of the old law. First, it seems that the conditions which had to be satisfied before a care or supervision order could be made may have acted as magnets: once they were satisfied the court proceeded to make an order without necessarily considering whether the order would actually improve the child's position [*Review of Child Care Law (1985), paragraph 15.22*]. Secondly, custody and access orders seem to have been made as a matter of course in matrimonial proceedings, as if they were part of the package which comes with maintenance or divorce [*Law Commission Report No. 172: Guardianship and Custody (1988), paragraph 3.2*]. There is no need for such orders in every case and it may be that they can polarise the attitudes of the individuals involved. It is hoped that section 1(5) will strengthen the welfare principle by underlining the need to justify an order being made.

Delay

3.23 The court must have regard to the general principle that delay in determining a question which relates to the upbringing of a child is likely to prejudice his welfare [*section 1(2)*]. This rule applies in any proceedings in which such a question arises, not just in proceedings under the Act. It recognises that a child's sense of time may be more acute than an adult's and that delay in determining the proceedings may in itself be harmful to the child. Where court proceedings about a child's upbringing are pending, it puts stress on all those involved which may rub off generally in damage to the child [*B v.B.[1985] F.L.R. 166,185*]. In a dispute over who is to care for a child who is living with one parent or is in the interim care of a local authority, delay may decide the case by tipping the balance in favour of maintaining the *status quo*.

3.24 The principle in section 1(2) is designed to encourage the courts to take steps to reduce the delay in children's cases. In Parts II and IV of the Act the court is required to draw up a timetable for the case to avoid delay and may give directions to ensure that the timetable is kept to [*sections 11(1) and 32*]. In these Parts the court considers questions relating to section 8 orders and local authority care and supervision. In such proceedings rules of court may make provision to avoid delay, for example by requiring that a party discloses to the others information about his case by a certain time. Where a guardian *ad litem* is appointed in a case, the rules will require him to assist the court in avoiding delay (*paragraph 3.114*).

3.25 Delay may be less harmful if time is spent seeking agreement through conciliation so that contested court proceedings are avoided. The principle in section 1(2) should not prevent exploration of room for agreement. It is directed at avoiding delay which will have no compensating benefit for the child.

FURTHER DUTIES OF COURTS IN MATRIMONIAL PROCEEDINGS

3.26 Although, as is explained below (*paragraph 3.30*), some court orders may be made in family proceedings without a prior application for them, usually an order will be in response to an application. In certain matrimonial proceedings, however, the court is required to consider whether to exercise its powers under the Act with respect to 'children of the family'. These are proceedings:

(a) for divorce, judicial separation and nullity of marriage under the Matrimonial Causes Act 1973 [*section 41 of that Act, as substituted by paragraph 31 of Schedule 12*]; and

(b) for financial relief between spouses under the Domestic Proceedings and Magistrates' Courts Act 1978 [*section 8 of that Act, as substituted by paragraph 36 of Schedule 13*].

3.27 The new duties replace those which existed under the old law. A child is 'a child of the family' if he is a child of both spouses or has been treated by them as a child of their family, unless he is placed with them as foster parents by a local authority or voluntary organisation [*section 52(1) of the 1973 Act and section 88(1) of the 1978 Act*]. A significant change is made in proceedings under the

1973 Act, where the duty of the court to be satisfied that the arrangements for the children are satisfactory or the best that can be devised in the circumstances is repealed. That duty is thought to have been unwarrantedly stringent, difficult for the court to carry out thoroughly and to have encouraged the making of unnecessary orders [*Law Commission Report No. 172: Guardianship and Custody (1988), paragraphs 3.5–3.11*]. Under the Children Act parents will retain parental responsibility for their children after separation or divorce (*paragraphs 2.22 et seq*).

3.28 In future in divorce and other proceedings to which section 41 of the 1973 Act applies, a hearing before a judge will not usually be required in each case. The spouses concerned will be encouraged to make joint statements of arrangements which they propose for the children [*as suggested by the Matrimonial Causes Procedure Committee ('the Booth Committee') in their Report in 1985*]. These statements will be considered by a registrar, possibly together with a court welfare officer, to assess whether an order may be required. However, as under the old section 41, the court will be able to hold up the decree absolute of divorce or nullity or the decree of judicial separation in rare cases. It may do so if it needs more time to consider whether or not to exercise its powers under the Act with respect to a child of the family and there are exceptional circumstances which make it in the interests of a child of the family to hold up the decree [*section 41(2), as amended by Schedule 12*]. It will seldom be in their interests to delay the decree because usually it is only after such decrees that the questions about the family housing can be resolved.

3.29 One of the powers which the court in matrimonial proceedings may wish to exercise is to direct the local authority to investigate the child's circumstances. It may make such a direction where it appears to the court that a care or supervision order may be appropriate. This power may also be exercised in any other family proceedings [*section 37*] (*see paragraphs 3.76–3.79*).

COURT ORDERS

3.30 The primary orders which may be made under the Act in family proceedings are as follows:

(a) Under Part I the court may give parental responsibility to a father who would otherwise not have it. It may also appoint a guardian for a child where a parent with parental responsibility for him or another guardian of his has died. These powers were considered in Chapter 2. They may be exercised on application to the court and the appointment of a guardian may also be made by a court of its own initiative (i.e. 'of its own motion') in other family proceedings, if it thinks it appropriate [*sections 4(1) and 5(1) and (2)*].

(b) Part II confers power to make 'section 8 orders'. This term refers to residence, contact, specific issue and prohibited steps orders. Each of these orders may be made on application or by the court of its own motion in family proceedings [*section 10(1) and (2)*]. Additionally, section 16 gives the court in family proceedings power to make family assistance orders and Schedule 1 permits applications to be made for financial orders with respect to children.

(c) Under Part IV applications may be made by a local authority or any authorised person for a care or supervision order. In relation to such applications the court may make interim care and supervision orders. Where a child is in care, orders may be made under section 34 (either on application or by the court of its own motion) with respect to contact with the child. Under section 36 of the Act a local education authority may apply for an education supervision order. Under section 37 the court in family proceedings may direct a local authority to investigate the child's circumstances.

3.31 The following paragraphs describe the circumstances in which orders may be made under Parts II and IV of the Act. (*Paragraphs 3.93–3.109 deal with the legal effect of orders in more detail*).

Section 8 Orders

3.32 These orders are defined by section 8(1) as follows:

"'a contact order' means an order requiring the person with whom a child lives, or is to live, to allow the child to visit or stay with the person named in the order, or for that person and the child otherwise to have contact with each other;

'a prohibited steps order' means an order that no step which could be taken by a parent in meeting his parental responsibility for a child, and which is of a kind specified in the order, shall be taken by any person without the consent of the court;

'a residence order' means an order settling the arrangements to be made as to the person with whom a child is to live; and

'a specific issue order' means an order giving directions for the purpose of determining a specific question which has arisen, or which may arise, in connection with any aspect of parental responsibility for a child."

3.33 Section 8 orders replace the powers of the courts to make custody and access orders and to resolve disputes between parents and others who have custody orders. They comprise a flexible package of orders which should be able to cater for any question which may arise about the welfare of a child. Each section 8 order may be made for a specified period, impose conditions on those affected by it and contain directions as to how it is to be carried into effect [*section 11(7)*]. A section 8 order may also be made during the proceedings when the court is not able to dispose finally of the proceedings (what are commonly called interim orders) [*section 11(3)*].

3.34 Section 8 orders are designed to provide practical solutions to questions which arise. Unlike the old law, the emphasis is not on the custodial or non-custodial status of a parent. The intention is to encourage the adults involved to maintain their involvement in the child's life and to avoid driving unnecessary wedges between them. Nevertheless, where a dispute has arisen the court is given extensive powers to resolve it.

3.35 An order may be made at any time until the child's eighteenth birthday but only exceptionally once he is 16 [*section 9(7)*]. An order varying or discharging a section 8 order may be made when the child is 16 or 17 even if the circumstances are not exceptional.

3.36 Contact orders may be used to decide what used to be questions of 'access'. However, contact is capable of meaning more than the face-to-face experience of access and, for example, may involve other forms of communication such as telephone calls or letters. Residence orders may be made in favour of more than one person even when those people do not live together. If so, the order may specify the periods during which the child is to live in the different households concerned [*section 11(4)*]. Such an order might be expressed in general terms (for example that these periods be as agreed by those involved) or more precisely.

3.37 Specific issue and prohibited steps orders will enable courts to make orders about particular matters on the application of any person with a *bona fide* interest in the child's welfare. As such these orders should reduce the need to apply for the exercise of the inherent jurisdiction of the High Court (in particular wardship) for this purpose. Where a contact or residence question arises, however, and it can be resolved by a contact or residence order, a specific issue or a prohibited steps order cannot be made simply to achieve the effect of a residence order or a contact order [*section 9(5)(a)*].

Who may apply?

3.38 The Act distinguishes between those who are entitled to apply for a section 8 order directly and those who may only do so with the prior permission (or 'leave') of the court [*section 10(1)(a) and (2)*].

3.39 Certain people are able to apply without leave as they are usually closely connected with the child. The child's parents and any guardian or person in whose favour a residence order is in force are entitled to apply for *any* section 8 order [*section 10(4)*].

3.40 Residence or contact orders (but not specific issue or prohibited steps orders) may be applied for without leave by a wider class of people [*section 10(5)*]:

(a) a step-parent (a party to a marriage in relation to whom the child is a child of the family [*this phrase is defined in section 105(1) to have the same meaning as in the matrimonial statutes*] (*see paragraph 3.27 above*)];

(b) a person with whom the child has lived for at least three years out of the last five [*The period need not have been continuous but must not have ended more than three months ago, section 10(10)*];

(c) any person who:

(i) where the child is subject to a residence order, has the consent of each of those in whose favour the order was made;

(ii) where the child is in care, has the consent of the local authority in whose care the child is; or

(iii) in any other case, has the consent of those who have parental responsibility for the child.

In addition, rules of court may entitle further categories of people to apply without leave [*section 10(7)*]. This power would be exercised if it seemed that the hurdle of leave was an unnecessary one in respect of such people (for example, if leave was always granted to them).

3.41 With the limited exceptions listed in paragraph 3.46, anyone else can apply for a section 8 order with leave ('an open door policy'). The open door policy recognises that any genuinely concerned person should be able to ask a court to consider a question which has arisen about a child's welfare. In extreme circumstances this may be the only way that a child can be protected [*for example Re D [1976] Fam. 185, where an educational psychologist asked a court to override a mother's agreement to her daughter's sterilisation*].

3.42 Leave to apply for an order will generally be granted if it is in the child's best interests to do so. The Law Commission commented that the "requirement of leave is intended as a filter to protect the child and his family against unwarranted interference in their comfort and security, while ensuring that the child's interests are properly respected" [*paragraph 4.41 of their Report*].

3.43 With leave, a child may himself apply for a section 8 order which affects him if he has sufficient understanding to make the application [*section 10(8)*]. Except in the case of a child-applicant, the court must have regard to the following factors when considering whether or not to grant leave [*section 10(9)*]:

(a) the nature of the proposed application for the section 8 order (such as whether the application is a genuine response to the child's welfare);

(b) the applicant's connection with the child (does this justify his seeking a Court order?);

(c) whether the child might be harmed by the disruption which the proposed application could make to his life (perhaps because of the stress the proceedings will have on the person caring for the child);

(d) where the child is being looked after by a local authority, the authority's plans for the child's future and the wishes and feelings of the child's parents. This factor will be particularly relevant where a local authority foster parent is seeking leave: it is important to maintain the confidence of the child's parents in the authority's child care service and of the authority themselves in their ability to plan for the child's future (*see also paragraph 3.46 below, which explains the circumstances in which the foster parent may apply*).

3.44 The Law Commission summarised the way in which they foresaw the leave process working. They said that "leave will scarcely be a hurdle at all to close relatives... who wish to care for or visit the child", but that otherwise "there will hardly ever be a good reason for interfering in the parents' exercise of their responsibilities unless the child's welfare is seriously at risk from their decision to take, or more probably not to take, a particular step, and only the people involved in taking that step for them would have the required degree of interest (the obvious example is medical treatment)" [*paragraph 4.41 of their Report*]. An order for costs will be available as a sanction against unwarranted applications and the court is given power to prohibit further applications (*paragraphs 3.110 and 3.111, below*).

3.45 Where it comes to variation and discharge of section 8 orders, generally the same rules about entitlement and leave apply [*see section 8(2)*]. In addition, anyone who is named in a contact order and any other person who successfully applied for a section 8 order may apply to vary or discharge the order in question [*section 10(6)*].

3.46 The open door policy means that the right to apply for section 8 orders is generally unfettered. However, section 9 imposes the following restrictions which apply to certain children who have been looked after by a local authority:

(a) where a child is in care, the only section 8 order which may be made in respect of him is a residence order. The court has power to make orders about contact with children in care under section 34. Specific issue and prohibited steps orders may not be made when a child is in care [*section 9(1)*]. By 'care' is meant under a care order, (*see paragraph 5.3*);

(b) an application for a residence or contact order may not be made by a local authority [*section 9(2)*]. And those orders may not be made in favour of a local authority. Instead, the local authority may apply under Parts IV and V of the Act to obtain compulsory powers regarding where the child should live or in order to see the child (*paragraph 3.48 below and chapter 6*). A local authority may apply for a specific issue or prohibited steps order if a child is not in care but these orders cannot be made so as to give a local authority parental powers with respect to a child or to achieve any of the other objectives which are denied to a court exercising the High Court's inherent jurisdiction with respect to children [*section 9(5)((b)*]. (*These restrictions, which are designed to prevent a child being placed in local authority care other than under Part IV, are explained in paragraphs 3.118–3.123*);

(c) a person who has been a local authority foster parent of a child within the last six months may not *apply for leave* unless he has the local authority's consent, he is a relative of the child or the child has lived with him for three out of the last five years [*section 9(3)*]. This period need not be continuous [*section 9(4)*]. A foster parent will be entitled to apply for an order without leave if he satisfies section 10(4) or (5) (*see paragraphs 3.39 and 3.40 above*). For example, if he has looked after the child for the last three years, he will not need leave to apply for a residence or contact order [*section 10(5)(b)*].

3.47 These restrictions follow from the special considerations which arise when a local authority is or has been involved (*see paragraphs 3.119–3.123 and the cases cited there*). The result is that generally the Act does not restrict the use of section 8 orders when a child is simply being accommodated by a local authority (and is not in their 'care'). A specific issue order might be sought in such a case to resolve a dispute over the child's education or medical treatment; or an order for contact with the child might be made in favour of a child's parent. This relaxes the old law under which it seemed that a court could not make orders in respect of a child who was in voluntary care if the local authority disagreed [*W v. Nottinghamshire County Council [1986] FLR 565*]. However, the restrictions mentioned in (b) and (c) of the previous paragraph still apply in these cases, so that the authority themselves may not apply for a residence or contact order and a foster parent in certain circumstances cannot apply without the consent of the local authority. The Act also requires the court to have regard to the local authority's plans for the child and the wishes and feelings of the child's parents if an application for leave to apply for a section 8 order is made (other than by the child) in respect of a child who is being looked after by a local authority [*section 10(9)(d)*].

Care and Supervision Orders

3.48 Care and supervision orders are the two main public law orders. The former places the child into the care of a local authority and the latter puts him under the supervision of a local authority or a probation officer [*section 31(1)*]. They are mutually exclusive [*section 91(3) and Schedule 3, paragraph 10*]. Similar orders to these could be made under a variety of statutes, principally the Children and Young Persons Act 1969. One of the most confusing aspects of child law was that, with no apparent logic, these orders were made according to different criteria and with different effects under the various statutes. The Children Act wipes the slate clean so that only one sort of care or supervision order may be made in the circumstances set out in section 31(2). [*A different kind of supervision order may be made in criminal proceedings under the Children and Young Persons Act 1969*]. Their legal effect is also streamlined (*see paragraphs 3.93–3.97 below*).

3.49 Care and supervision orders under the new law may only be made on the application of a local authority or an authorised person [*section 31(1)*]. The National Society for the Prevention of Cruelty to

Children (hereafter referred to as the NSPCC) and its officers are authorised for this purpose and the Secretary of State has power to authorise others [*section 31(9)*]. Before applying for a care or supervision order an authorised person should consult the local authority for the area where the child usually lives, if it is reasonably practicable to do so [*section 31(6)*]. Authorised persons may not apply in certain circumstances, such as where the child is already subject to a care or supervision order [*section 31(7)*]. The right of the police and local education authorities to seek orders under the 1969 Act is not preserved. (Local education authorities may apply for an education supervision order, *paragraphs 3.80–3.83 below*). A care or supervision order may not be made when the child has reached 17 (or 16 if married) [*section 31(3)*].

3.50 Neither a care nor a supervision order may be made unless the conditions in section 31(2) are satisfied. These are:

(a) that the child concerned is suffering, or is likely to suffer, significant harm; and

(b) that the harm, or likelihood of harm, is attributable to –

(i) the care given to the child, or likely to be given to him if the order were not made, not being what it would be reasonable to expect a parent to give to him; or

(ii) the child being beyond parental control.

3.51 Even when a court is satisfied of the above conditions, a care or supervision order will not necessarily follow. The court has to proceed to apply the principles which govern its decision-making in all proceedings under the Act. These are discussed in paragraphs 3.13–3.25 above.

3.52 The conditions in section 31(2) express in statutory language the principles set out by the Review of Child Care Law in 1985. The first condition reflects the view that "the primary justification for the state to initiate proceedings seeking compulsory powers is actual or likely harm to the child" [*paragraph 15.12 of the Review*]. The child must be shown to be suffering or likely to suffer a substantial deficit in the standard of health or development which it is reasonable to expect him to achieve [*paragraph 15.14 of the Review*]. 'Harm' in section 31(2) includes both:

(a) ill-treatment (which includes sexual abuse and non-physical ill-treatment such as emotional abuse), and

(b) the impairment of health or development [*section 31(9): health means physical or mental health and development means physical, intellectual, emotional, social or behavioural development.*]

3.53 A child may have particular needs, such as for specific health care or emotional support, which it is reasonable to expect to be met. If they are not, and his health or development are impaired, he could be said to be suffering 'harm'.

3.54 To satisfy the first condition, the harm must be shown to be 'significant'. Minor short-comings in health or development should not give rise to compulsory intervention [*paragraph 15.15 of the Review*]. Where ill-treatment is proved, it should not be difficult to find that the child is suffering significant harm. However, when assessing whether the impairment of health or development is significant, the court must compare the health or development of the child in question with that which could be expected of a similar child, that is a child with similar attributes and needs [*section 31(10)*]. The comparison with the health or development of a hypothetical similar child should enable the court to decide both whether the child before it is achieving or will achieve the standard of health or development which it is reasonable to expect for him and, if he is not, whether the deficit is significant.

3.55 The second condition is that the harm suffered, or the likelihood of harm to be suffered, is attributable to the absence of a reasonable standard of parental care. Only where there is such an absence should the state be able to step in to take over parental responsibility for the child [*paragraph 15.23 of the Review*]. An absence of a reasonable standard of parental care need not imply that the parents are at fault. It may arise because the child's parents are not able or willing to provide a reasonable standard of care or because the child himself is beyond their control and rejects the care they would like to provide. In both situations the standard of parenting which a child is expected to receive is an objective one. The child's parents are judged by what a reasonable parent would do for the child in question.

3.56 The test is not what can reasonably be expected of the child's parents in their circumstances and given their characteristics. If a parent is not able to provide a reasonable standard of care, he is expected to seek the help of others to ensure that such care is provided. For example, usually it would be reasonable in the interests of the child to expect a parent who is unable to provide adequate food, shelter or health care and whose child is suffering significant harm to turn to the assistance available from family or friends or from public authorities or voluntary agencies. If the child's parents decline to do so, it could be said that their standard of parenting falls below that which it is reasonable to expect of them.

3.57 Proceedings under Part IV are 'family proceedings' so that any section 8 order may be made in them as an alternative to a care or supervision order (*paragraph 3.30*). An example would be of a residence order made in favour of a relative of the child who is willing to care for him. Section 8 orders may also be combined with supervision orders (but not care orders [*section 9(1)*]). Where an application for a care order is made, the court may decide to make a supervision order instead (and *vice versa*) [*section 31(5)*].

Interim Care and Supervision Orders

3.58 Where an application has been made for a care or supervision order there will usually be a period of time before the court is in a position to decide which order, if any, to make. Under the Children and Young Persons Act 1969 the court could only make an interim care order in these circumstances (but not an interim supervision order) and the grounds on which such orders were made were not clearly established. Under the Children Act the court may make one of the following orders during this period:

(a) any section 8 order (subject to the restrictions which usually apply to these orders), which, as explained in paragraph 3.33 above, may be made for a specific period; an example would be a residence order which is not to last beyond the date on which the application before the court is determined;

(b) an interim care order, or

(c) an interim supervision order [*section 38(1)*].

3.59 The last two orders are similar in effect to full care and supervision orders. The differences are explained in the next paragraph. They may not be made simply because they are thought to be desirable. The court must be satisfied that there are reasonable grounds for believing that the conditions in section 31(2) are fulfilled [*section 38(2)*]. Even if so satisfied, the court will apply the principles discussed above (*paragraphs 3.13–3.25*) and may decide to make a section 8 order instead or no order at all. However, if a residence order is made, the court must also make an interim supervision order, unless it is satisfied that the child's welfare will be satisfactorily safeguarded without it [*section 38(3)*]. This rule acknowledges that where a local authority is seeking a care or supervision order and the court chooses to make a residence order at the interim stage, the court should have to consider carefully whether the child will be sufficiently protected without an interim supervision order.

3.60 The essential differences between interim and full care and supervision orders are that in the former case the court may make certain directions and the duration of the orders is more restricted. Otherwise the powers and responsibilities of local authorities under these orders are the same (*paragraphs 3.100–3.103 and chapter 5*).

3.61 When an interim order is made (or at any time thereafter while the order is in force) directions may be given as to the medical or psychiatric examination or other assessment of the child [*section 38(6) and (8)(a)*]. Where, for example, a social work assessment will have to be undertaken to find out whether suspected abuse or neglect has taken place, the court may make directions controlling the way in which this work is to be carried out, including requiring that a joint assessment takes place where both a local authority and the child's parents wish to carry out similar investigations. If it thinks that certain examinations or assessments would be harmful to the child, the court may direct that they should not take place (either at all or unless it otherwise directs) [*section 38(7)*].

3.62 By making such directions the court should be able to protect the interests of the child concerned as well as of the other parties to the proceedings. Directions will also assist the court to control the timetable which must be set in these proceedings to avoid unnecessary delay (*paragraphs 3.23–3.25*). The court may later vary directions which have been made [*section 38(8)(b)*]. In contrast, the court has no power to make directions when it makes a full care order and, in the case of full supervision orders, its powers are more circumscribed (*paragraph 3.101*). A child who is of sufficient understanding to make an informed decision may refuse to submit to an examination or assessment [*section 38(6)*].

3.63 The duration of interim care and supervision orders may be specified by the court, which will have regard to the general principles in paragraphs 3.13–3.25 [*section 38(4)*]. In contrast, the court may not impose limits on the duration of full care and supervision orders (except where a supervision order is extended). (See paragraph 3.102 below). When considering how long an interim order should endure the court must consider whether any party who was, or might have been, opposed to the making of the order was in a position to argue his case against the order in full [*section 38(10)*]. Where, for example, a parent has not had sufficient time to instruct a lawyer in the proceedings, the court may decide to make a short interim order so that the parent can be properly represented at an early next hearing.

3.64 The rules in section 38(4) impose long-stops beyond which interim orders may not last. The first interim order may last for no longer than eight weeks [*section 38(4)(a)*]. Any later order cannot last for more than four weeks except where the first order itself was made less than four weeks ago [*section 38(4)(b) and (5)(a)*]. In those circumstances the second (or later) order may go on up to a date eight weeks after the first order was made [*section 38(4)(b) and (5)(b)*]. For example, if a court makes a first interim order lasting two weeks, it may make a second lasting for six weeks. If the first two interim orders last for one week each, the third may last for six weeks. However, where the first order lasts for four weeks, any later order can only last for a maximum of four weeks. Where the application for a full order is disposed of (i.e. an order is granted or the proceedings are dismissed or withdrawn) any interim order ceases to have effect [*section 38(5)(c) and (d)*]. In the case of an interim order which is made when the court has directed an investigation by a local authority (*see paragraph 3.79 below*), the order will also cease to have effect at the end of the period fixed by the court (if any) for the local authority to report to it, if no application for a full order has been made in that time [*section 38(5)(e)*].

Contact under Section 34

3.65 Before a child is placed in local authority care under a full or interim care order the court must consider the arrangements the local authority have made, or propose to make, for contact between the child and other people, in particular the child's parents and other interested relatives [*section 34(11)*]. The court will invite the parties to the proceedings to comment on these arrangements. Local authorities' duties to promote contact will be considered further in Chapter 5 (*paragraphs 5.25–5.27*). Here, the courts' powers to make orders regarding contact are set out. Unlike the old law which gave limited power to make orders when access by specific people had been refused or terminated, section 34 enables the court to consider questions about contact with any person and to make directions about the kind or amount of contact which should be allowed.

3.66 Contact orders when a child is in care are dealt with in section 34 rather than section 8. Section 34(1) requires reasonable contact to be allowed between a child in care and the following people:

(a) his parents;

(b) his guardian, if any;

(c) where there was a residence order in force before the care order was made, the person in whose favour the order had been made; and

(d) where, before the care order was made, a person had care of a child by virtue of an order made in the exercise of the High Court's inherent jurisdiction with respect to children, that person.

3.67 Subject to any court order, it is for the authority to decide how much contact is reasonable in all the circumstances. The authority may only refuse reasonable contact with the child to one of those listed above where they have the court's authority or in an emergency. The authority are encouraged to allow contact with people outside that list, such as relatives or friends of the child (*paragraphs 3.25–3.27*), but do not need prior authority to refuse their contact with the child, where the authority consider that contact would not be in the child's interests. Their parental responsibility for a child in care would allow them to restrict contact in such cases.

3.68 With this background in mind, the court is not given a simple power to regulate contact (as is provided in respect of section 8 orders for children who are not in care). Instead, the range of orders about contact which are available to the court are more specific:

(a) if one of the people listed above is unhappy about the contact which is allowed by the local authority, they may ask the court to make a contact order in their favour [*section 34(3)(a)*];

(b) the child or the local authority may apply for the authority to be authorised to refuse contact between the child and one of those listed above (i.e. despite the presumption of contact, the order may result in no contact being allowed) [*section 34(4)*];

(c) the child or the local authority concerned may apply for an order about the contact which is to be allowed between the child and any person named in the order (who may or may not be a person in the above list) [*section 34(2)*];

(d) any other person may seek leave to apply for an order regarding the contact which is to be allowed between the child and himself [*section 34(3)(b)*].

Any of these orders may be made by the court in family proceedings of its own motion (without an application having been made) [*section 34(5)*]. Orders about contact may be made subject to conditions, such as that contact should be restricted to defined occasions or places, or should be for a temporary period [*section 34(7)*]. They may also be varied or discharged on the application of the child, the local authority or the person named in the order [*section 34(9)*].

3.69 In an emergency, for up to seven days, the authority may refuse to allow contact which would otherwise be required either by virtue of a court order or the presumption in section 34(1) [*section 34(6)*]. They may only do so if satisfied that the refusal is necessary to safeguard or promote the child's welfare and where the refusal was decided upon as a matter of urgency.

Variation and Discharge of Care and Supervision Orders

3.70 A care order may be discharged on the application of the local authority, the child concerned or any person who has parental responsibility for him [*section 39(1)*]. A supervision order may be varied (by the imposition or modification of requirements or the extension of its duration, (*paragraphs 3.100–3.103 below*)), or discharged on the application of the supervisor, the supervised child or a person with parental responsibility for him [*section 39(2)*]. Where a person does not have parental responsibility for the child, such as a foster parent or relative, he may apply for a residence order in his favour, which, if granted, will either automatically discharge the care order or entitle him to apply to vary or discharge the supervision order (*paragraph 3.95 below*), subject to the rules which restrict the right to apply for section 8 orders, (see paragraphs 3.38–3.47 above).

3.71 Variation of a supervision order entails the court adding to, modifying or deleting one of the requirements which may be imposed under such an order. As will be explained below (*paragraphs 3.100–3.103*), such requirements may be imposed on any person with whom the child is living (whether or not he has parental responsibility for the child). Where such a person is subject to requirements he also may apply to have the supervision order varied [*section 39(3)*].

3.72 Where a child is in care, a person who is entitled to apply for the order to be discharged may ask the court to substitute a supervision order for the care order [*section 39(4)*]. The court may do so even if it could not be said that the conditions in section 31(2) (which must be satisfied before a supervision order is made) are established [section 39(5)]. Unlike under the Children and Young Persons Act 1969, however, a supervision order may not be converted to a care order unless the conditions are satisfied.

Orders Pending Appeal

3.73 Rules of court will define who may appeal against decisions made by courts under the Act. Unlike under the old law, the local authority, the child and his parents will be able to appeal against decisions about care and supervision orders. In limited circumstances care and supervision orders may be made to protect the child while an appeal is made. Such orders pending appeal may be made subject to directions of the court, for example regarding the residence of the child or the duration of the order [*section 40(1)–(4)*]. They may not last beyond the determination of the appeal or, where no appeal is made, the period during which an appeal could have been made [*section 40(4) and (6)*]. They are intended to maintain protection for the child which would otherwise cease. These orders are:

(a) a care order which may be made if the court dismisses an application for a care order and at the time of dismissal the child is the subject of an interim care order [*section 40(1)*];

(b) a supervision order which may be made if the court dismisses an application for a care or supervision order and at the time of dismissal the child is the subject of an interim supervision order [*section 40(2)*].

3.74 If a court grants an application to discharge a care or supervision order it may order that the discharge should not have effect or that the care or supervision order should continue in force subject to directions [*section 40(3)*].

3.75 Appeals may be made against the decision of a court in respect of an order pending appeal. The appellate court may extend the duration of the care or supervision order which is in question if such an appeal is made or if an application is made to it in connection with a proposed appeal [*section 40(5)*].

Referral to the Local Authority

3.76 A court which is hearing family proceedings in which a question arises about the welfare of a child may direct a local authority to investigate the child's circumstances if it appears that a care or supervision order may be appropriate [*section 37(1)*].

3.77 A direction requires the local authority to consider whether to take any action with respect to the child, such as applying for a care or supervision order or providing services or assistance to the child or his family [*section 37(2)*]. If the authority decide not to apply for a care or supervision order they must report their decision to the court, giving their reasons and details of any action (including the provision of services or assistance) they are taking or propose to take with respect to the child [*section 37(3)*]. This information must be provided within eight weeks of the direction, unless the court otherwise directs [*section 37(4)*]. They must also consider whether the child's circumstances should be reviewed and, if so, decide when that review should begin [*section 37(6)*].

3.78 This power to direct a local authority investigation replaces the power of most courts in family proceedings to make a care or supervision order of their own motion 'in exceptional circumstances'. Under the Act a care or supervision order may only be made when the local authority or an authorised person has applied for either such order. Care and supervision orders place such important responsibilities on local authorities that it is left to them to decide, taking into account the circumstances identified in their investigation, whether or not to apply for an order. Moreover, it will be for them to decide what other services may be provided to the family which might preclude any order being made.

3.79 Following a direction by a court in family proceedings, if the authority decide to apply for a care or supervision order, they will usually make that application before the court which made the direction. While the local authority are carrying out an investigation under a direction, the court may make an interim care or supervision order to safeguard the child's welfare [*section 38(1)(b)*]. These interim orders may be made subject to the rules set out in paragraphs 3.58–3.64 above.

Education Supervision Orders

3.80 The Act creates a new kind of supervision order which may be made on the application of a local education authority. Education supervision orders appoint a designated local education authority to secure that the child receives proper education [*section 36(1) and (7)*]. They may only be made where the condition in section 36(3) is satisfied: that the child is of compulsory school age and is not being properly educated (i.e. he is not receiving efficient full-time education suitable to his age, ability and aptitude and any special educational needs he may have [*section 36(4)*]).

3.81 The condition in section 36(3) used to be one of the conditions satisfaction of which could lead to a care or supervision order being made under the Children and Young Persons Act 1969 [*section 1(2)(e) of that Act*]. Just as under that Act, unless the contrary is proved, it is presumed that a child is not being properly educated where he is the subject of a school attendance order which has not been complied with or he is not attending regularly a school at which he is a registered pupil [*section 36(5)*]. Unlike the position under the 1969 Act, failure to educate a child properly is not in itself sufficient to enable the court to make a care order. However, such failure may be evidence on which the court is prepared to find that the child is suffering significant harm, since 'harm' is defined to include the impairment of development (whether it be physical, intellectual, emotional, social or behavioural development) (paragraph 3.52 above).

3.82 Where a local education authority propose to apply for an education supervision order, they must first consult the social services committee or a nominated officer of the relevant local authority [*section 36(8) and (9), under which the relevant authority will usually be the one within whose area the child is living or will live*]. After consultation it should be possible to decide whether it would be appropriate for the local authority to provide services under Part III of the Act or to apply for a care or supervision order themselves under Part IV (*see chapter 4 regarding local authority services and Chapter 6 for the authority's duty to investigate the child's circumstances*). An education supervision order may not be made while a child is subject to a care order [*section 36(6)*].

3.83 An education supervision order may be discharged on the application of the local education authority, the child concerned or any parent of his [*Schedule 3, paragraph 17(1)*]. The effect of an education supervision order is considered further in paragraphs 3.104–3.109 below.

Family Assistance Orders

3.84 A court may make a family assistance order in family proceedings where it has power to make an order under Part II of the Act and there are exceptional circumstances [*section 16(1) and (3)(a)*]. Under a family assistance order a local authority or probation officer will be made available to give advice and assistance to (and, where appropriate befriend) a person named in the order [*section 16(1)*]. The person or persons named in the order may be the child himself, a parent or guardian of his or any person with whom the child lives or in whose favour a contact order is in force with respect to the child [*section 16(2)*]. Before an order may be made each person named in it (except the child) must have given his consent [*section 16(3)(b)*].

3.85 A family assistance order is a short term order. It may only last for up to six months [*section 16(5)*)]) and is designed to give expert help to families. It will be particularly useful where there has been separation or divorce and a family needs assistance to cope with problems arising during what may be a difficult period of transition. In part this new order replaces the supervision order which could be made under the old law in divorce and other family proceedings. Unlike those supervision orders, family assistance orders may be made even if the court makes no other order in respect of the child. They may be used to promote cooperation within the family so that, for example, arrangements for contact with the child may be established, even if no order as to contact has been made. If a section 8 order has been made with respect to the child and the officer providing the assistance thinks that it should be varied or discharged, he may bring the case before the court [*section 16(6)*].

3.86 Most family assistance orders will probably appoint a probation officer to carry them out. Probation officers (acting as divorce court welfare officers) will usually have had involvement with the family when compiling a welfare report. However, where a local authority has worked with the family or has compiled the report, one of their officers might be a more appropriate appointment. The order may require a person named in it to assist the officer involved by informing him of the address of named persons and allowing him to visit them [*section 16(4)*].

Financial Orders under Schedule 1

3.87 Schedule 1 of the Act confers comprehensive powers to make orders for financial assistance of children. These powers replace, powers conferred by the Guardianship Acts 1971–1973 and the Children Act 1975 and the Family Law Reform Act 1987 [*Schedule 1 also makes provision for the alteration of maintenance agreements, paragraph 10*]. The main features of the new powers are that:

(a) they may be exercised by a court on the application of a parent, a guardian or a person in whose favour a residence order is in force with respect to the child [*Schedule 1, paragraph 1(1)*];

(b) they require payment to be made by a parent [*Schedule 1, paragraph 1(2)*];

(c) the powers may be exercised at any time [*Schedule 1, paragraph 1(3). When a court makes a residence order, a financial order may be made even though no application has been made, paragraph 1(6)*];

(d) although existing powers to make orders for the benefit of children remain available in proceedings relating to marriage [*under the Matrimonial Causes Act 1973 and the Domestic Proceedings and Magistrates' Courts Act 1978*], the courts' powers are generally as extensive under the Children Act as they are in those proceedings;

(e) the same orders under the Act may be made in respect of children of married and unmarried parents;

(f) proceedings under Schedule 1 are classed as 'family proceedings', so that orders may be made about the care of the children concerned [*Schedule 1 is within Part II of the Act: section 15*].

3.88 With the limited exception of children who have reached 18 years old, a 'parent' of a child in this context includes any party to a marriage (whether or not it is subsisting) in relation to whom the child concerned is a 'child of the family' [*Schedule 1, paragraph 16*]. This means that a person may apply for, or be made to pay under, an order in respect of a child who is not his own, but who has been treated by himself and his spouse (or ex-spouse, as appropriate) as a child of the family [*unless the child was placed with them as foster parents, section 105(1)*].

3.89 The orders which may be made are for periodical payments (secured or unsecured), a lump sum payment, transfer of property and settlement of property [*Schedule 1, paragraph 1(2), although a magistrates' court may not make orders for transfer or settlement of property or for secured periodical payments, paragraph 1(1)*]. Payment or transfer may be to the child himself or to the applicant on behalf of the child. Periodical payments orders may be varied or discharged on the application of payer and payee [*Schedule 1, paragraph 1(4)*]. Further periodical payments and lump sum orders may be made, although only one transfer or settlement of property order may be made against the same person in favour of the same child [*Schedule 1, paragraph 1(5)*]. A child who has reached 16 may apply for the variation of a periodical payments order which has been made for his benefit [*Schedule 1, paragraph 6(4)*]. A periodical payment or lump sum order may be applied for by a child who has reached 18 if he is or will (or would) be in education or training or there are special circumstances [*Schedule 1, paragraphs 2 and 6(5)*].

3.90 When considering whether to make a financial order under Schedule 1, the court must have regard to the all the circumstances. The child's welfare is not the paramount consideration, although the presumption of no order applies so that an order may not be made unless to do so would be better for the child than not making it [*section 1(4)*]. The court must balance the interests of all those involved and, in particular, must consider [*Schedule 1, paragraph 4*]:

(a) the income, earning capacity and resources which the applicant, the child (if he is not the applicant) and any parent of his, have or are likely to have in the foreseeable future [*'parent' has the wide meaning given by paragraph 16 of the Schedule*];

(b) the financial needs, obligations and responsibilities which those people have or are likely to have in the foreseeable future;

(c) any physical or mental disability of the child;

(d) the manner in which the child was being, or was expected to be educated or trained.

3.91 If an application is made against a person who is not the mother or father of the child, the court must also take into account whether that person has assumed responsibility for the child and, if so, to what extent, on what basis and for how long he has done so. It will also be relevant whether he knew that the child was not his child and what liability any other person has for the child [*Schedule 1, paragraph 4(2)*].

3.92 Periodical payments orders may run from the date on which the application was made or from any later date specified by the court [*Schedule 1, paragraph 3(1)*]. Such orders will only go on beyond the child's 17th birthday if the court so specifies and may not last beyond his 18th unless the child is or will (or would) be in education or training or there are special circumstances [*Schedule 1, paragraph 3(1) and (2)*]. Periodical payments orders which are not secured cease to have effect on the death of the payer [*Schedule 1, paragraph 3(3)*]. Orders (other than those under paragraph 2) also cease to have effect where the two parents who are payer and payee live together for a period of more than six months [*Schedule 1, paragraph 3(4)*].

THE EFFECT OF COURT ORDERS

3.93 The effect of orders on parental responsibility was explained in the previous chapter (see paragraphs 2.22–2.26). The following paragraphs explain more detailed rules which apply to certain orders.

Duration

3.94 Subject to the exceptions listed below, orders last until the child's 18th birthday unless they are discharged earlier by the making of another court order [*section 91(7), (11) and (12)*]. The same applies to parental responsibility agreements under section and the appointment of guardians under section 5 [*section 91(8)*]. The exceptions to this rule are as follows:

(a) section 8 orders may be made for a limited period or to cease in specified circumstances [*section 11(7)*];

(b) section 8 orders will cease to have effect when the child reaches *sixteen* unless the court has ordered otherwise, which it may only do if the circumstances of the case are exceptional [*section 9(6) and (7) and section 91(10) and (11)*];

(c) where a residence order has been made in respect of a child under which he is to live with one of two parents who each have parental responsibility for him, the order will cease to have effect if the parents live together for a continuous period of more than six months [*section 11(5)*];

(d) where a contact order requires the parent with whom a child lives to allow the child to have contact with his other parent, the order will cease to have effect if the parents live together for a continuous period of more than six months [*section 11(6)*];

(e) supervision and education supervision orders are brought to an end under the rules set out in paragraphs 3.102 and 3.108 below;

(f) interim care and supervision orders cease to have effect according to the rules in paragraphs 3.63 and 3.64;

(g) the special rules governing financial orders under Schedule 1 were explained in paragraph 3.92.

3.95 A care order discharges any existing section 8 order [*section 91(2)*]. It also brings to an end an existing wardship where the child was a ward of court when the care order was made [*section 91(4)*]. If an emergency protection order is made while a child is in care, the care order has effect subject to the later order [*section 91(6)*]. A residence order discharges an existing care order. If the child is adopted any order under the Act will cease to have effect [*Adoption Act 1976, section 12(3), as amended by paragraph 3(3) of Schedule 10*].

Change of Surname

3.96 Where a residence or care order is in force with respect to a child, no one may take steps to cause him to be known by a new surname without either the written consent of every person who has parental responsibility or the leave of the court [*sections 13(1) and 33(7)*].

Leaving the United Kingdom

3.97 The same consents or the leave of the court are required before a child who is under a residence or care order may be taken out of the United Kingdom [*sections 13(1) and 33(7)*]. This rule does not apply to the person in whose favour the residence or care order was made who removes the child for a period of less than a month [*section 13(2) and 33(8)(a)*]. Where a residence order is made, the court may make a further order which prohibits the removal of the child even for one month (either as a condition of the residence order or as a specific issue or prohibited steps order). In the case of a care order, of course, it is the local authority who may remove the child and the court cannot prevent this by way of a condition or a section 8 order. There is no power to place conditions on care orders (*other than those made pending an appeal, paragraph 3.73*) and section 9(1) excludes specific issue and prohibited steps orders while a child is in care. However, if the local authority wish to arrange for a child in their care to *live abroad*, more detailed rules apply and they must seek the court's approval [*section 33(8)(b)*] (*see paragraph 5.23*).

Enforcement of Section 8 Orders

3.98 Where a person fails to give up a child in breach of a section 8 order, the court may authorise an officer of the court or a constable to take charge of the child and take him to the person in whose favour the section 8 order has been made [*section 34 of the Family Law Act 1986, as amended by Schedule 13*]. Such authority also includes authority to enter and search premises where the child is believed to be and to use force which is necessary to give effect to the order.

3.99 If a person is in breach of the requirements of a residence order, for example by keeping the child away from the person with whom the child is to live under the order, the order may be enforced by proceedings for contempt of court or, in a magistrates' court, under section 63 of the Magistrates' Courts Act 1980 [section 14].

Supervision Orders

3.100 A supervision order puts a child under the supervision of a local authority or a probation officer [*Schedule 3, paragraph 9*]. The supervisor is required to advise, assist and befriend the child and to take steps which are reasonably necessary to give effect to the order [*section 35(1)*]. Regulations may be made concerning the exercise of a supervisor's functions by a local authority [*Schedule 3, paragraph 11(1)*]. The Children Act breaks new ground by imposing obligations not only on the supervised child but also on 'a responsible person', who may be a person who has parental responsibility for the child or any other person with whom the child is living [*Schedule 3, paragraph 1*]. A responsible person is required to inform the supervisor of the child's address (if he knows it and is asked) and, if he is living with the child, to allow the supervisor reasonable contact with the child [*Schedule 3, paragraph 8(2)*]. A search warrant may be sought if contact is refused (*paragraph 6.54–6.55*).

3.101 A supervision order may also require any of the following things:

(a) that the supervised child should keep the supervisor informed of his address and allow the supervisor to visit him where he is living [*Schedule 3, paragraph 8(1)*]. (*Again, for the availability of search warrants, see paragraphs 6.54–6.55*);

(b) that the responsible person should keep the supervisor informed of his address if it differs from the child's [*Schedule 3, paragraph 3(3)*];

(c) that the supervised child should comply with any directions given by the supervisor which require him to:

   (i) live at a specified place for a specified period; (but not with a specified person, which would require a residence order)

   (ii) present himself to a specified person at a time and place specified;

   (iii) participate in specified activities as specified [*Schedule 3, paragraph 2(1)*].

Directions enable a supervisor to require a child to undergo education or training and to receive counselling and guidance as well as to take part in local schemes such as those known as 'intermediate treatment', although directions may not be given relating to medical or psychiatric examination or treatment (see (g) below). Directions may be given at the discretion of the supervisor and may be varied by him [*Schedule 3, paragraph 2*].

(d) with his consent, a responsible person may be required by the order to take all reasonable steps to ensure that the child complies with directions under (c) above or (f) or (g) below [*Schedule 3, paragraph 3(1) (a) and (b)*];

(e) also with his consent, the responsible person may be required to comply with a direction to attend at a specified place and time to take part in specified activities [*Schedule 3, paragraph 3(1)(c)*]. The child may also be directed to attend. The purpose of directions under (e) may be to provide services to the responsible person (such as training in parenting skills) or to require him to attend a clinic or a hospital with the child for check-ups (see (f) and (g) below).

Directions given by a supervisor under the above powers may not require compliance for more than 90 days in total [*disregarding days of non-compliance, Schedule 3, paragraph 7*].

(f) that the child should submit to a medical or psychiatric examination (either a particular examination or as directed by the supervisor). Such an examination may be as an in-patient if a registered medical practitioner satisfies the court that it is necessary and that the child may be suffering from a condition which requires, and may be susceptible to, treatment [*Schedule 3, paragraph 4*].

(g) that the child should submit to medical or psychiatric treatment for a period specified in the order. A requirement to this effect may only be included where the court is satisfied on the evidence of a registered medical practitioner (who is approved under the Mental Health Act 1983 in the case of psychiatric treatment) that the child's condition requires, and may be susceptible to, treatment [*Schedule 3, paragraph 5(1) and (3)*]. (Also in the case of psychiatric treatment, the child's condition must not be such as would warrant his detention under a hospital order). A medical practitioner is required to report to the supervisor if the treatment is no longer required; should be changed or should continue beyond the length of the order; the child is not susceptible to treatment; or he is himself unwilling to continue to be responsible for the child's treatment [*Schedule 3, paragraph 5(6)*]. Such a report should be referred to the court [*Schedule 3, paragraph 5(7)*].

Requirements under (f) and (g) may not be imposed unless satisfactory arrangements have been, or can be, made for the examination or treatment and, where the child is of sufficient understanding to make an informed decision, he consents to it [*Schedule 3, paragraphs 4(4) and 5(5)*]. Requirements under (f) and (g) may not be included in a interim supervision order, under which the court has different direction-making powers [*section 38(9)*] (see paragraph 3.61 above).

3.102 A supervision order terminates an earlier care or supervision order (but not a supervision order made in criminal proceedings or an education supervision order) [*Schedule 3, paragraph 10*]. At first, it only lasts for one year, although the supervisor may apply to extend the order, or further extend it, for a period of up to three years from when it was made. A supervision order cannot last beyond the child's eighteenth birthday [*Schedule 3, paragraph 6*].

3.103 The supervisor is required to consider whether to apply for the variation or discharge of a supervision order if it is not complied with in full or if he thinks that the order may no longer be necessary [*section 35(1)(c)*].

Education Supervision Orders

3.104 The supervisor under an education supervision order is required to advise, assist and befriend, and give directions to, the child concerned and his parents in such a way as will, in his opinion, secure that the child will be properly educated [*Schedule 3, paragraph 12(1)*]. In giving directions he must take into account the wishes and feelings of the child and his parents (where it has been reasonably practicable to obtain them), in particular as to the place at which the child should be educated [*Schedule 3, paragraph 12(2) and (3)*]. 'Parent' in this context has the wide meaning given in education legislation: it includes a person with parental responsibility for the child as well as anyone else who has care of him [*Schedule 3, paragraph 21 and section 114(1D) of the Education Act 1944, as inserted by paragraph 10 of Schedule 13*].

3.105 An education supervision order may require the child to keep the supervisor informed of his address and to allow the supervisor to visit him [*Schedule 3, paragraph 16(1)*]. It also requires a parent who is living with the child to allow the supervisor reasonable contact with him and to inform the supervisor of his address, if it is different from the child's [*Schedule 3, paragraph 16(2)*].

3.106 If a supervisor's directions are not complied with, he should consider what further steps he should take [*Schedule 3, paragraph 12(1)(b)*]. The options include making new directions, referring the child's case to the local authority and applying for discharge of the education supervision order [*Schedule 3, paragraphs 12(4), 17 and 19*]. If an order is discharged, the court may direct the local authority to investigate the child's circumstances [*Schedule 3, paragraph 17(2)*].

3.107 The child's parents are required to comply with the supervisor's directions [*Schedule 3, paragraph 13(1)*]. Persistent failure to comply is an offence, although a number of defences are provided, such as that the parent took all reasonable steps to comply [*Schedule 3, paragraph 18*]. If the child persistently fails to comply with a direction, the local education authority must notify the local authority, who should investigate the child's circumstances [*Schedule 3, paragraph 19(2)*]. The authority will consider whether to provide services to the child or his family and whether an application should be made for an order under the Act.

3.108 An education supervision order lasts for one year, although the local education authority may apply for an extension (not earlier than three months before the order would expire). Each extension may last for up to three years. In any case, the order ceases to have effect if a care order is made or the child ceases to be of compulsory school age [*Schedule 3, paragraph 15*].

3.109 An education supervision order may run concurrently with a supervision order or a criminal supervision order. If so, a failure to comply with the direction of the education supervisor should be disregarded if it would not have been reasonably practicable to comply with it without failing to comply with a direction given under either of the other orders [*Schedule 3, paragraph 14*]. However, if an earlier criminal supervision order contained requirements as to the child's education, those requirements will cease to have effect when the education supervision order is made [*and if a further criminal supervision order is made such requirements as to the child's education may not be imposed: Schedule 3, paragraph 13(2)(c) and (d).*]. An existing school attendance order is also discharged by the making of an education supervision order [*and a new one cannot be made: Schedule 3, paragraph 13(2) (a) and (b)*].

PROHIBITIONS ON APPLICATIONS

3.110 In family cases applications are occasionally made repeatedly with no prospect of success. The court may act to prevent the hardship this may cause the other people involved, including the child, by prohibiting applications being made with respect to the child concerned by the person named in the order without the leave of the court [*section 91(14)*].

3.111 In proceedings under Part IV there is also a general bar on making further applications with respect to the child concerned without the court's leave [*section 91(15) and (17)*]. This bar lasts for six months from the disposal of the previous application where that application was for:

(a) the discharge of a care, supervision or education supervision order [*but not interim orders, section 91(16)*]. The bar also applies in respect of applications for child assessment orders, (*see paragraph 6.40*);

(b) the substitution of a supervision order for a care order;

(c) an order regarding contact under section 34 and that application was refused.

The bar applies to further applications by *any* person, except in the case of (c) where it only applies to the person who made the previous application. In the cases of (a) and (b) the bar applies to future applications for any of the orders referred to in (a) and (b).

GUARDIANS *AD LITEM* AND WELFARE REPORTS

3.112 The following independent reports remain available to the court:

(a) in any proceedings in which the court is considering a question with respect to the child under the Act, it may ask a probation officer (who is usually a court welfare officer) or a local authority to provide a report on the child's welfare or specific matters relating to that child's welfare [*section 7(1)*]. The local authority may arrange for the report to be provided by one of its officers or another appropriate person (but not a probation officer). The report may be in writing or oral, as the court requires [*section 7(3)*]. Unlike in proceedings under the Children and Young

Persons Act 1969 and the Children Act 1975, a local authority report is not required unless the court so orders. Regulations may be made about the content of such reports [*section 7(2)*].

(b) in certain proceedings a *guardian ad litem* must be appointed for the child unless the court is satisfied that it is not necessary to do so to safeguard the child's interests [*section 41(1)*]. These proceedings relate to care and supervision orders (but not education supervision orders) and to orders under Part V of the Act (principally emergency protection and child assessment orders) [*section 41(6)*]. The guardian will represent the child, instruct a solicitor for him in accordance with rules of court and will report to the court [*section 41(2)*].

(c) the High Court may ask the Official Solicitor to provide a report [*section 41(8)*]. Appropriately trained members of the Official Solicitor's staff will be encouraged to join local panels of guardians *ad litem*. Where a member of his staff is appointed guardian *ad litem*, that member will be bound by the same rules as apply to other panel guardians, including the rules which require the appointment of a solicitor for the child.

3.113 Guardians *ad litem* will be appointed from panels established by local authorities. As under the old arrangements, local authorities will be responsible for the payment of fees, allowances and expenses of guardians. However, in order to clarify the independence of a self-employed guardian from the local authority involved in the proceedings in which he is appointed, more joint arrangements between local authorities for panels will be encouraged (and may be required) [*section 41(7) and (9)*].

3.114 Rules of court will require guardians to be appointed earlier than they often were under the old law. For the first time they may be appointed where emergency proceedings are taken to protect the child (under Part V). It is intended that the guardian will be able to play a role throughout the proceedings, so that, for example, he may advise the court about the making of interim orders, or about questions relating to contact with the child, directions about the examination or assessment of the child and directions which may be made to ensure that a timetable is adhered to in order to avoid unnecessary delay. The guardian should also be able to take an active role in the proceedings by applying for directions to be made or for interim orders to be discharged if they are no longer needed [*section 41(10)*].

3.115 Where a report is made by a guardian *ad litem* or an officer under (a) in paragraph 3.112, statements in the report and any evidence given in respect of the matters referred to in the report will always be admissible in evidence, even if a rule of law (such as the hearsay rule) would otherwise exclude it [*sections 7(4) and 41(11)*].

3.116 Guardians *ad litem* are given the right to examine and take copies of two kinds of local authority records [*section 42*]. The first are records which are held by the local authority and were compiled in connection with the bringing of proceedings under the Act with respect to the child. The second are other records which relate to the child concerned and were compiled under the functions of the social services department [*under Schedule 1 of the Local Authority Social Services Act 1970*]. The copies taken will always be admissible as evidence of any matter referred to in either the guardian's report or in evidence which the guardian gives in the proceedings (even if there is otherwise a rule of law which excludes it) [*section 42(2) and (3)*].

LEGAL REPRESENTATION OF THE CHILD

3.117 In most family proceedings, as under the old law, the child will not be legally represented, although rules will give the court power to appoint a solicitor to represent him where a question under the Act arises *(for the power of the child to make applications for section 8 orders, see paragraph 3.43)*. However, in proceedings in which a guardian *ad litem* should be appointed, the Act lays down rules under which the legal representation of the child should always be considered by the guardian (if any) and the court and which should result in the child having legal representation where it is appropriate. Where a guardian is appointed he will be under a duty to instruct a solicitor unless the court otherwise directs *[under rules of court, section 41(2)]*. Where no solicitor has been appointed, however, the court may appoint one if it would be in the child's best interests to do so; or no guardian *ad litem* has been appointed; or the child has sufficient understanding to instruct a solicitor and wishes to do so *[section 41(3) and (4)]*. In that last case, of course, there will be nothing to prevent a child from appointing his own solicitor, if he so chooses.

WARDSHIP AND THE INHERENT JURISDICTION OF THE HIGH COURT

3.118 The Children Act for the most part leaves untouched the inherent jurisdiction of the High Court (the most frequently used vehicle for which is wardship). The future of wardship itself was considered during the Law Commission's Review of Child Care Law *[Working Paper No. 101 (1987)]*. The Commission decided to postpone its conclusion about the need for an additional jurisdiction regarding children until the effect of the Children Act can be assessed. The Children Act incorporates many of the beneficial features of wardship, such as the 'open door policy' and a flexible range of orders, and it is likely that the use of that jurisdiction will decline.

3.119 The Government thought it necessary to restrict local authorities' use of the inherent jurisdiction (in particular, wardship) where the Act provides appropriate remedies. Otherwise the controls which the Act imposes, such as the conditions which must be satisfied before public law orders (in particular care, supervision, emergency protection and child assessment orders) may be made and the restrictions which are put on these orders (such as on their duration and other effects) would be undermined. Section 100(2) therefore prohibits the inherent jurisdiction being used as an alternative to the public law orders which are available under the Act. In particular:

"No court shall exercise the High Court's inherent jurisdiction with respect to children –
(a) so as to require a child to be placed in the care, or put under the supervision, of a local authority;
(b) so as to require a child to be accommodated by or on behalf of a local authority;
(c) so as to make a child who is the subject of a care order a ward of court; or
(d) for the purposes of conferring on any local authority power to determine any issue which has arisen, or which may arise, in connection with any aspect of parental responsibility for a child."

3.120 Where the wardship court thinks that a care or supervision order may be needed, it may direct a local authority to investigate the child's circumstances and, if the statutory conditions are satisfied, make an interim care or supervision order. These are the same powers which are available to any court in family proceedings (*paragraphs 3.76–3.79*). Similarly, since proceedings under the inherent jurisdiction are 'family proceedings', a section 8 order may be made in them [*section 8(3)*]. (*paragraph 3.30 above*).

3.121 The Act also affects the relationship between wardship and local authority care. Under the old law, it was possible for a child in compulsory care also to be a ward of court. Wardship in these circumstances could only be invoked with the concurrence of the local authority under the principles set out in the cases of *A v. Liverpool City Council* and *Re W [[1982] A.C.363 and [1985] A.C.791]*. An exception to this arose where a ward of court was committed to care under section 7(2) of the Family Law Reform Act 1969 and the court retained power to give directions to the local authority on the application of others, such as the child's parents. While the child was a ward the local authority's powers were uncertain because, in wardship, the court is said to be the child's guardian. The authority's powers were restricted by the rule which requires that major decisions in the ward's life should be referred to the court. Where a child is in care this division of responsibility for the child should not occur. The local authority has parental responsibility for the child and should be able to take whatever decisions are necessary.

3.122 The Act therefore makes wardship and care incompatible. If a ward of court is committed to care, the wardship ceases to have effect [*section 91(4)*]. While a child is in care, he cannot be made a ward [*section 100(2) and section 41 of the Supreme Court Act 1981, as amended by paragraph 45 of Schedule 13*].

3.123 The inherent jurisdiction of the High Court apart from wardship remains available to deal with specific matters which may arise even when a child is in care. The court may deal with the application without the panoply of wardship being invoked. The exercise of the inherent jurisdiction will be subject to two limitations. The first is the rule in *A v. Liverpool City Council* mentioned above (which effectively precludes orders being made against the wishes of the local authority when the authority are exercising their statutory functions in relation to the child in question). The second limitation prevents a local authority applying for the exercise of the inherent jurisdiction without the leave of the court [*section 100(2)*]. Leave may only be granted when the conditions in section 100(4) are satisfied, namely:

(a) the authority could not achieve the desired result through the making of any order other than one under the inherent jurisdiction [*the local authority may be able to achieve the desired result by applying for an order under Parts IV or V of the Act or, where the child is not in care, by applying for a section 8 order*]; and

(b) there is reasonable cause to believe that the child is likely to suffer significant harm if the inherent jurisdiction is not exercised.

These conditions will prevent the local authority from using the inherent jurisdiction as an alternative to the statutory scheme and limit their ability to seek compulsory powers in respect of a child to cases in which he might otherwise suffer significant harm [*'significant harm' has the same meaning as in Part IV of the Act, section 105(1)*] (*see paragraphs 3.54 and 3.55*). In this way the Act attempts to keep the balance between the interests of family autonomy and child protection.

3.124 Civil legal aid will be available for proceedings under the Act and will thus come within the scope of the Legal Aid Board. In order that the Board can grant legal aid swiftly, the merits test will be waived for those who are automatically parties to applications for care and supervision orders (including the child) and legal aid will be granted in advance of the means test on an emergency basis [*section 99*].

TRANSITIONAL PROVISIONS

3.125 Schedule 14 makes detailed transitional provisions regarding orders made under the old law. In brief, the most important of these provisions are as follows.

3.126 Proceedings which are pending under the old law at the time the Act comes into force will continue unaffected by the new law [*Schedule 14, paragraph 1(1)*]. For certain exceptions, see the remainder of that paragraph].

3.127 Existing orders regarding custody, legal custody, care and control and access continue to have effect after the Act comes into force. The fact that a person has parental responsibility for a child under the Act does not mean that he may act incompatibly with an existing order [*paragraphs 6(3) and 7(3)*].

3.128 A person who otherwise would not have parental responsibility for the child but who had care and control or custody of a child under an existing order is given parental responsibility while that order lasts. Thus, a father who does not have parental responsibility for his child because he is not married to the child's mother, but who had care and control or custody under an existing order, is deemed to have a 'parental responsibility order' in his favour [*paragraph 6(4)*]. (*paragraphs 2.6–2.8*) Any other person who had custody or care and control by virtue of an existing order, and who is not a parent or guardian of the child, is given parental responsibility for the duration of the existing order [*paragraph 7(1)*]. Such a person (for example a 'custodian' under the Children Act 1975) is also treated in specific instances as if he had the benefit of a residence order [*he may apply for a section 8 order without leave, for example, and, if he had care and control of the child (rather than custody without care and control), certain other provisions apply: paragraphs 7 and 8*]. A person with an access order under the old law is not given parental responsibility but is treated for certain purposes in the Act as if he had a contact order [*paragraph 9*].

3.129 Existing orders regarding custody, legal custody, care and control and access may be discharged by a court, either on application or of its own motion in family proceedings [*paragraph 11(3)*]. They are also brought to an end if the court makes a residence or care order under the Act [*paragraph 11(1)*].

3.130 Children under care orders made under the old law (for example under the Children and Young Persons Act 1969) are treated as if they had been made subject to a care order under section 31 of the Act. The same applies to children who were subject to a parental rights resolution [*paragraph 15*]. Where a court has made directions to the local authority (under powers which have been repealed), these directions are preserved and may be varied or discharged [*paragraph 16(5)*]. Orders for access to a child in care (made under the Child Care Act 1980) are treated as contact orders under section 34 of the Act [*paragraph 18*].

3.131 Supervision orders under the repealed provisions in the Children and Young Persons Act 1969 are treated as supervision orders under section 31 [*paragraph 25(2)*]. The new rule in the Act which restricts the duration of supervision orders to an initial period of one year is applied to old supervision orders, with modification to allow the local authority time to apply for extension of an order which would have endured for more than one year under the old law [*paragraphs 25(3)–(5)*].

3.132 Supervision orders made under repealed provisions in divorce and other family proceedings are preserved for a maximum period of one year from commencement of the Act [*paragraph 26*].

CHAPTER 4 <u>LOCAL AUTHORITY SERVICES FOR CHILDREN AND FAMILIES</u>

4.1 Part III of the Children Act draws together local authorities' principal functions in respect of children. It consists of a range of new duties, which include the identification of children who are in need, support of children's links with their families, the provision of day care and the setting up of procedures to consider representations about the provision of services. It also restates in a modified form functions towards children which existed under the Child Care Act 1980, the National Assistance Act 1948 and Schedule 8 of the National Health Service Act 1977. In future, the scope of local authority social services functions under the 1948 and 1977 Acts in respect of disabled people is restricted to adults. Apart from the Children Act, only the Chronically Sick and Disabled Persons Act 1971 and the Disabled Persons (Services, Consultation and Representation) Act 1986 continue to confer additional functions in respect of children. [With the exception of Schedule 8, paragraph 2, of the National Health Service Act 1977, which relates to the care of mothers of babies and young children, including where the mothers are themselves under eighteen.]

CHILDREN IN NEED

4.2 The Children Act identifies a class of children who are the primary target of local authority functions under Part III. These are 'children in need'. A child is in need if:

"(a) he is unlikely to achieve or maintain, or to have the opportunity of achieving or maintaining, a reasonable standard of health or development without the provision for him of services by a local authority under this Part;

(b) his health or development is likely to be significantly impaired, or further impaired, without the provision for him of such services; or

(c) he is disabled".

[*Section 17(11): 'development' means physical, intellectual, emotional, social or behavioural development; and 'health' means physical or mental health.*]

4.3. A child is disabled "if he is blind, deaf or dumb or suffers from mental disorder of any kind or is substantially and permanently handicapped by illness, injury or congenital deformity or such other disability as may be prescribed." [Section 17(11)]. The word disabled has the same meaning as it has in the National Assistance Act 1948 in respect of adults. Services for disabled children are integrated with those which are provided for other children in need. This means that, where they are provided with accommodation by local authorities, disabled children benefit from the powers and duties which local authorities have in respect of all children whom they look after. Under the old law, they did not so benefit unless they were "received into care" [*under section 2 of the Child Care Act 1980*].

SAFEGUARDING AND PROMOTING CHILDREN'S WELFARE

4.4 Of major importance is the general duty of each local authority to provide a range and level of services which are appropriate to the needs of children in their area who are 'in need' so as to:

(a) safeguard and promote the welfare of such children; and

(b) so far as is consistent with that aim, promote their upbringing by their families [*section 17(1)*].

4.5 By 'family' is not meant only blood relatives: any person who has parental responsibility for the child and any other person with whom he has been living is included [*section 17(10)*]. Services may be provided to the family of a child in need, rather than specifically to the child, if they are provided with a view to safeguarding and promoting the child's welfare [*section 17(3)*].

4.6 Local authorities are required to facilitate the provision by others (in particular voluntary organisations) of services which they provide under Part III [*section 17(5), with the exception of secure accommodation, reviews and representations procedures under sections 25 and 26*]. Authorities may also arrange for others to act on their behalf in the provision of these services (for example in the provision of day care and fostering services).

4.7 The general duty to provide services is supported by the more specific duties in Part III. In particular, the first Part of Schedule 2 of the Act confers a series of functions on local authorities. This Part of the Schedule may be amended or added to by the Secretary of State in response to developments in child care work [*section 17(4)*]. The principal duties are set out in paragraphs 4.8 to 4.18 below:

Identification and Assessment

4.8 Local authorities must take reasonable steps to identify the extent to which there are children in need in their area [*Schedule 2, paragraph 1(1)*]. They must also publish information about services provided and take reasonable steps to ensure that those who may benefit from services receive the information which is relevant to them [*Schedule 2, paragraph 1(2)*].

4.9 A register of disabled children within the area must be kept [*Schedule 2, paragraph 2*].

4.10 An assessment of the needs of a child who is in need may be carried out at the same time as an assessment under other relevant legislation, such as the Chronically Sick and Disabled Persons Act 1970, the Education Act 1981 or the Disabled Persons (Services, Consultation and Representation) Act 1986 [*Schedule 2, paragraph 3*].

Prevention

4.11 Reasonable steps must be taken through the provision of services to prevent children in the area suffering neglect or ill-treatment [*Schedule 2, paragraph 4(1)*]. There is a connected duty to take reasonable steps to reduce the need to bring:

(i) proceedings which may result in care or supervision orders being made in respect of children in their area;

(ii) criminal proceedings against such children;

(iii) proceedings under the inherent jurisdiction of the High Court in respect of such children.

4.12 Local authorities must take reasonable steps to encourage children in their area not to commit criminal offences. They must also take such steps to avoid the need for them to be placed in secure accommodation [*Schedule 2, paragraph 7*].

4.13 In individual cases local authorities are required to investigate the circumstances of children who may be at risk and may have to seek compulsory powers to remove such children from their homes. They may also assist a person to find alternative accommodation if he is likely to ill-treat a child who is living on the same premises [*Schedule 2, paragraph 5*]. These functions are considered further in paragraphs 6.3–6.9.

4.14 Where a local authority believe that a child within their area is likely to suffer harm and lives or proposes to live in the area of another local authority, they must inform that local authority, specifying the harm which he may suffer and, if possible, where he lives or will live [*Schedule 2, paragraph 4(2) and (3)*].

Family Support

4.15 For children in need who live with their families, the local authority must provide as they consider appropriate for the following services to be available: advice, guidance and counselling; activities; home help (including laundry facilities); assistance with travelling to use a service provided under the Act (or a similar service); assistance to enable the child and his family to have a holiday [*Schedule 2, paragraph 8. Activities may be occupational, social cultural or recreational*].

4.16 For any children in the area, the local authority must provide family centres as they consider appropriate. A family centre is a centre at which the child, his parents, any other person who has parental reponsibility for him and any other person who is looking after him may attend for activities or advice, guidance or counselling (during which time they may be provided with accommodation) [*Schedule 2, paragraph 9*].

4.17 For a child in need who is living away from his family, the local authority must take such steps as are reasonably practicable to enable him to live with his family or to promote contact between him and his family, if it is necessary to do so to safeguard or promote his welfare. This duty does not apply where the child is being looked after by the local authority, when additional duties are imposed [*Schedule 2, paragraph 10*]. (*For these additional duties, see paragraphs 5.22–5.27*).

Disabled Children

4.18 Services must be provided to minimise the effect on disabled children in the area of their disabilities and to give such children the chance to lead lives which are as normal as possible [*Schedule 2, paragraph 6*].

ASSISTANCE

4.19 Local authorities may give assistance in kind or, in exceptional circumstances, in cash in the exercise of their functions [*section 17(6)*]. Unlike under the old law, this assistance may be made conditional on whole or partial repayment [*section 17(7)*]. Before giving assistance or imposing conditions, the authority must have regard to the means of the child and his parents [*section 17(8)*]. A person is not liable to repay while he is in receipt of income support or family credit [*section 17(9)*].

4.20 Local authorities may also contribute to the cost of looking after a child who is living with a person under a residence order, except where that person is a parent or step parent of the child [*Schedule 1, paragraph 15. This provision replaces the power to make payments to a 'custodian' of a child under the Children Act 1975*].

4.21 The Act imposes new duties on local authorities to provide day care. A local authority must provide appropriate day care for children in need in their area who are aged five or under and not yet attending schools [*section 18(1)*]. They must also provide appropriate care and supervised activities outside school hours and during school holidays for children in need in their area of any age who are attending school [*section 18(5)*]. They also have power to provide either of these services for children in their area who are not in need [*section 18(2) and (6)*]. When arranging for day care the local authority must take into account the different racial groups to which children in their area who are in need belong [*Schedule 2, paragraph 11*].

4.22 'Day care' is defined as any form of care or supervised activity provided for children during the day (whether or not it is provided on a regular basis) [*section 18(4)*]. 'Supervised activities' are those which are supervised by a responsible person [*section 18(7)*]. A local authority may provide training, advice, guidance, counselling and other facilities for those who care for children in day care or who accompany children while they are in day care [*section 18(3)*].

4.23 The Act also requires each local authority to review (together with the appropriate local education authority) the provision of day care and other services described in paragraphs 4.21 and 4.22 [*section 19(1) and (2)*]. The review should cover additionally the extent to which day care and child minding services are available in the area for children under eight from other persons who must register such facilities under Part X of the Act. The review must also take into account the provision of facilities for under-eights in schools, hospitals and other establishments which are exempt from registration under Part X [*section 19(4) and (5)*]. (*For these establishments, see paragraph 7.5*).

4.24 The first reviews must be carried out within one year of section 19 being brought into force. Subsequent reviews must take place in every three year period beginning with the anniversary of the commencement of section 19 [*section 19(2) and (5)*]. Reviews may also be held at other times. In conducting a review regard should be had to representations made by a health authority and any other relevant representations which have been made [*section 19(7)*]. The results of each review must be published as soon as is reasonably practicable together with any proposals which there may be on the subject of the review [*section 19(6)*].

4.25 A local authority in Scotland must review the extent to which child minders are available for under-eights and to which they and those registered under Part X provide day care within their area [*section 19(3)–(8) applies also in Scotland*]. The only difference from English and Welsh authorities is that there is no duty to consult the education authority.

ACCOMMODATION

4.26 A local authority must provide accommodation for a child in need in their area who requires accommodation as a result of—

"(a) there being no person who has parental responsibility for him;

(b) his being lost or having been abandoned; or

(c) the person who has been caring for him being prevented (whether or not permanently, and for whatever reason) from providing him with suitable accommodation or care." [*section 20(1)*]

This duty replaces the duty to receive a child into 'voluntary care' in similar circumstances [*section 2 of the Child Care Act 1980*] and the status of voluntary care is abolished. If the child who is accommodated under this duty is ordinarily resident in the area of another local authority, the latter authority may take over the provision of accommodation for the child within three months of being notified in writing that the child is being accommodated [*section 20(2). In such cases, whether or not notification takes place or provision of accommodation is taken over, the former authority may recover reasonable expenses from the latter, section 29(7)*]. A local authority is also required to provide accommodation for a child in need who has reached 16 if his welfare is otherwise likely to be seriously prejudiced [*section 20(3)*].

4.27 A local authority is *empowered* to provide accommodation for any child in their area if it would safeguard or promote his welfare [*section 20(4)*]. In the same circumstances an authority may accommodate in a community home any person who has reached 16 but is under 21, provided that the home takes children who have reached 16 [*section 20(5)*]. (*A community home is defined in paragraph 5.17.*)

4.28 The type of accommodation which may be provided under these functions is described in the next chapter. Children who are accommodated are referred to as 'looked after' by the local authority. Accommodation is provided on a voluntary basis. It may not be provided if a person who has parental responsibility for the child objects and is able and willing to provide (or arrange for the provision of) accommodation for the child [*section 20(7)*]. Similarly a person with parental responsibility for the child may at any time remove him from accommodation which has been provided [*section 20(8)*]. There are two exceptions to these rules.

4.29 First, they do not apply if a person in whose favour a residence order is in force with respect to the child agrees to the provision of accommodation; or if a person who has care of the child under an order made in the exercise of the High Court's inherent jurisdiction with respect to children [*section 20(9)*]. If more than one person has the benefit of a residence order or has care of the child under an inherent jurisdiction order, all of them must agree to the child being looked after by the local authority [*section 20(10)*]. If the parent who has a residence order in his favour agrees to the provision of accommodation, the other parent cannot object to it being provided or remove the child. If he wished to take over care of the child he would have to get the residence order discharged.

4.30 The second exception is that if the child has reached sixteen, accommodation may be provided in the face of parental objection, provided that the child agrees to it [*section 20(11)*].

4.31 Before accommodation is provided, so far as it is reasonably practicable and consistent with the child's welfare, the local authority must ascertain the child's wishes regarding the provision of accommodation and give due consideration to them (having regard to his age and understanding) [*section 20(6)*]. Regulations and guidance will stress the importance of written arrangements being made with the child, his parents or anyone else (such as a relative) who was looking after the child before the authority provided accommodation. These documents will set out (amongst other things) the purpose of the child's stay in local authority accommodation, the arrangements for contact with the child and any delegation of parental responsibility which may be necessary. They should explain that it will usually be in the child's interests for his return to be planned by all those concerned.

REPRESENTATIONS PROCEDURES

4.32 Each local authority is required to establish a procedure for considering representations (including complaints) about the discharge of their functions under Part III. This procedure must receive appropriate publicity [*section 26(8)*]. Representations may be made by any child who is looked after by the authority or any other child who is in need and any person who the authority consider to have a sufficient interest in the child's welfare to warrant his representations being considered by them. They may also be made by a parent of the child, any other person who has parental responsibility for him or a local authority foster parent [*section 26(3)*].

4.33 The representations procedure must have an independent element, which means that a person who is not a member or an officer of the authority must take part in the consideration of the representations and any discussions which are held about the action which is to be taken [*section 26(4)*]. Regulations will be made regarding the procedure which is to be followed by local authorities in considering representations [*section 26(5)*]. Local authorities will also be required to monitor their representations procedures to ensure that they comply with these regulations [*section 26(6)*].

4.34 Once the procedure has been completed, the local authority must have due regard to the findings of those who carried it out (although they are not bound to implement these findings). Reasonable steps should be taken to notify in writing the person who made the representation, the child (if he has sufficient understanding) and anyone else who is likely to be affected, of the authority's decision in the matter, their reasons and any action which has been or will be taken [*section 26(7)*].

CONTRIBUTIONS

4.35 Local authorities may recover charges for the services set out above, with the exception of advice, guidance or counselling. Charges for accommodation are dealt with in the next chapter (*paragraphs 5.31 and 5.32*).

4.36 Charges which the authority consider to be reasonable may be recovered from the parents of the child in receipt of the service, or, if the child is 16, the child himself [*section 29(1) and (4)*]. If a service is provided for a member of the child's family, that member may be charged [*section 29(4)*]. A person is not liable to pay a charge while he receives income support or family credit [*section 29(3)*]. If a person's means are insufficient to pay the charge, he may not be required to pay more than can be reasonably expected [*section 29(2)*].

CO-OPERATION BETWEEN AUTHORITIES

4.37 A local authority may request certain other persons to help in the exercise of their functions under Part III. These are any other local authority, a local education authority, a local housing authority, a health authority or any other person authorised by the Secretary of State. Authorities which receive a request for help (specifying the action which is wanted) must comply, provided that the request is compatible with their own statutory or other duties and does not unduly prejudice the discharge of any of their functions [*section 27*]. If a local authority comply with a request in respect of a child or other person who is not ordinarily resident in their area, they may recover reasonable expenses from the local authority for that area [*section 29(9)*].

4.38 A local authority must assist a local education authority with the provision of services for a child in their area who has special educational needs [*section 27(4)*].

CHAPTER 5 CHILDREN WHO ARE LOOKED AFTER BY LOCAL AUTHORITIES

5.1 This chapter explains the powers and duties of local authorities towards children whom they look after. It covers those provisions in Part III and Schedule 2 of the Act which were not explained in the previous chapter. Most of these provisions derive from the Child Care Act 1980, the whole of which is repealed. The Children Act makes a clearer distinction between the voluntary and compulsory powers of local authorities. The status of 'voluntary care' is abolished along with the power to assume parental rights by an administrative resolution. Compulsory powers may only be obtained by court order and even then parents retain their parental responsibility. A local authority's duty to make plans for children whom they look after is strengthened; the involvement of parents and others in decision-making is required, and after-care functions are also given new emphasis.

WHICH CHILDREN ARE 'LOOKED AFTER'?

5.2 A child is looked after by a local authority if he is in their care or provided with accommodation by the authority in the exercise of their social services functions [*section 22(1)*]. Accommodation means accommodation which is provided for more than 24 hours [*section 22(2). Social services functions are found in Schedule 1 of the Local Authority Social Services Act 1970, as amended by Schedules 13 and 15 of the Children Act*]. These circumstances will be taken in turn.

5.3 By 'care' is meant the care of a local authority under a care order [*section 105(1)*]. In addition children under certain other orders are deemed to be in care, for example where a child has been made subject to an order which is equivalent to a care order elsewhere in the United Kingdom, Channel Islands or the Isle of Man and is transferred to England and Wales [*by virtue of section 101*]. Care orders may only be made in the circumstances described in Chapter 3.

5.4 A care order gives the local authority parental responsibility for the child [*section 33(3)(a)*]. This order terminates any previous section 8 order which was in force with respect to him [*section 91(2)*]. However, any person who is a parent or guardian of the child retains parental responsibility for him and may exercise this responsibility independently of the authority, provided that he does not act incompatibly with the care order (such as by taking the child away from his placement without permission) [*section 2(8)*] (*see paragraphs 2.22–2.26*). For example, if, while the child is staying with him, a parent wants to take his child to visit a particular relative, he may do so, even if the local authority disapprove. However, the authority may prevent a parent or guardian from exercising his parental responsibility if it is necessary to do so to safeguard or promote the child's welfare [*section 33(3) and (4)*]. If, in the above example, the authority consider that seeing the relative in question was likely to put the child at risk, they could require the parent not to go through with his plan.

5.5 A local authority cannot use their power to determine the extent to which a parent may exercise his parental responsibility so as to restrict a person exercising his statutory rights [*section 33(9)*]. For example, a parent or guardian will remain entitled to withhold his agreement to a child's adoption or consent to his marriage [*section 33(6)(b) and, (for consent to marriage, see paragraph 8.10)*]. Also, a person will always be able to do what is reasonable in all the circumstances to safeguard or promote a child's welfare if he has care of him [*section 33(5) and section 3(5)*] (*see paragraph 2.27*).

5.6 Children who are accommodated by local authorities voluntarily are accommodated under section 20, which was discussed in the previous chapter (*paragraphs 4.26–4.31*). One of the most significant changes from the old law is that a child accommodated under this section (who used to be referred to as in 'voluntary care') will cease to be so accommodated if a person with parental responsibility removes him. Although local authorities are to be required to provide written details of their arrangements with parents and will be encouraged to reach agreements about the use of accommodation services, they may not *enforce* a period of notice before removal (*paragraph 4.28*). If the authority want to continue to look after the child against the wishes of a person who has the right to remove the child, they will have to seek a court order (or in an emergency they could ask a constable to take the child into police protection). Nevertheless, a person who is for the time being caring for a child should act to protect him from harm (such as by withholding him from a violent or drunken parent) [*section 1 of the Children and Young Persons Act 1933*.]. There is also an exception to the right of removal in the case of the older child. If a child is 16 and agrees to be accommodated by the local authority, they may accommodate him under section 20 against the wishes of his parents (*paragraph 4.30*).

5.7 An additional group of children are those who are compulsorily accommodated by local authorities. These are children on remand or the subject of a supervision order with a residence requirement and those children in police protection or who have been arrested whom the police ask the authority to receive [*section 21 (see paragraphs 6.30 and 8.11–8.15)*]. Local authorities are also required to arrange accommodation for children who are kept away from home under emergency protection and child assessment orders [*section 21(1)*] and when they do these children are also 'looked after'.

GENERAL DUTIES

5.8 The duties of local authorities towards children who are looked after have been strengthened by the Children Act. More emphasis is placed on the need to involve those people who are important in the child's life. Local authorities are required to take account of the wishes and feelings of all those who are relevant to a decision which is to be taken. They must also take steps to settle the child back with his family and to encourage contact with his family and others who are connected with him (unless either of these things would be contrary to the child's best interests).

The Welfare Duty

5.9 The cornerstone duty is that a local authority must safeguard and promote the welfare of each child whom they look after [*section 22(3) (a)*]. This duty replaces the more vague duty to give "first consideration" to the need to safeguard and promote the child's welfare [*section 18 of the Child Care Act 1980*]. As under the old law, the authority are required to make reasonable use (for the benefit of children who are looked after) of the services and facilities which are available for children cared for by their own parents.

Consultation

5.10 Before they take a decision with respect to a child whom they are looking after (or proposing to look after), the authority must, so far as is reasonably practicable, ascertain the wishes and feelings regarding the matter, of the child, his parents, any other person who has parental responsibility for him and any other person whose wishes and feelings they consider to be relevant [*section 22(4)*]. And when they come to make the decision, they must give due consideration to the wishes and feelings of those people (in the child's case, having regard to his age and understanding) [*section 22(5)*]. It will not always be practicable to ascertain the wishes and feelings of all those who are relevant. Where emergency action has to be taken to protect the child, or a person cannot be tracked down by taking reasonable steps, the consultation duties will not impede decision-making.

Religion, Racial Origin, Cultural and Linguistic Background

5.11 Local authorities must also give due consideration to the child's religious persuasion, racial origin and cultural and linguistic background [*section 22(5)(c)*]. These factors must be taken into account even if there has been insufficient time to investigate the wishes and feelings of the child and others.

Protection of the Public

5.12 In the unusual case of it being necessary to act to protect the members of the public from serious injury, the local authority may disregard their duties in the previous three paragraphs [*section 22(6)*]. In those circumstances, the Secretary of State may be able to give directions to the local authority about the care of the child (such as regarding where he should live) [*section 22(7)*].

ACCOMMODATION

5.13 A local authority may provide accommodation for a child by making one of the following arrangements. In each case the authority must maintain the child [*section 23(1)(b)*] and the placement may be regulated by the Secretary of State. The range of options are:

(a) a family placement;

(b) placement in a community, voluntary or registered children's home or a home provided by the Secretary of State;

(c) other appropriate arrangements [*section 23(2)*].

5.14 By 'a family placement' is meant placement with a family, a relative or another suitable person. Under the old law these placements were referred to as boarding-out and charge and control placements, depending on with whom the child was placed. Under the Children Act, a person with whom a child is placed is 'a local authority foster parent' unless he is:

(i) a parent;

(ii) any other person who has parental responsibility for the child (such as a guardian or a person in whose favour a residence order is in force with respect to the child); or

(iii) in the case of a child in care, any person in whose favour a residence order was in force immediately before the care order was made (such a person will have had parental responsibility for the child until the care order brought the residence order to an end) [*section 23(3) and (4)*].

5.15 If a child who is in care is placed with a person within (i)–(iii), the placement will be subject to regulations which derive from the Accommodation of Children (Charge and Control) Regulations 1988. If a child who is accommodated under section 20 (i.e. on the basis of voluntary arrangements) goes to live with such a person he will cease to be provided with accommodation by the local authority [*after-care functions under section 24 may apply*]. Other family placements will be subject to local authority fostering regulations, which derive from the Boarding-out of Children (Foster Placement) Regulations 1988. Unlike the old law, placements with relatives and friends of a child are classed as foster placements rather than the equivalent of home placements (or in the old terminology 'charge and control'), except where such a person has (or had, in the case of a care order child) parental responsibility for the child under a residence order.

5.16 In making arrangements for people to act as local authority foster parents, local authorities must take into account the different racial groups to which children in their area who are in need belong [*Schedule 2, paragraph 11*].

5.17 Local authorities are required to secure the availability of community homes under Part VI of the Act [*Section 53(1)*]. As under the old law, these homes may be:

(a) provided, managed, equipped and maintained by a local authority or a voluntary organisation (in the latter case the home is refered to as 'an assisted community home'); or

(b) provided by a voluntary organisation and managed, equipped and maintained by a local authority ('a controlled community home') [*section 53(3). Rules regarding the establishment of controlled and assisted homes are set out in Schedule 4.*].

5.18 Revised regulations will be prepared in respect of community homes. These will govern placements in community homes, the conduct of such homes and the welfare of children living in them.

5.19 Voluntary homes and registered children's homes are considered further in Chapter 7. A significant change from the old law is that where a person fosters more than three children who are not all siblings with respect to each other, unless he is exempted by the local authority, he will be treated as if he carried on a children's home, which must be registered as such (*paragraphs 7.24–7.27*). The intention is to ensure that the right regulations apply to the children living with that person. The process of exemption is considered further in Chapter 7.

5.20 The Secretary of State may arrange for homes to be provided for children who need particular facilities which are unlikely to be readily available in community homes [*section 82(5)*]. There are currently two of these homes, which are known as Youth Treatment Centres. Placements in such homes will not be subject to specific regulations. The Secretary of State, through those running the homes for him, sets the terms on which a child is maintained in them [*section 23(2)(e)*].

5.21 Paragraph 5.13(c) referred to a residual category of 'other arrangements' for children. These may include provision of hostels for semi-independent living or arrangements for rented accommodation to be provided for older children by suitable landlords.

THE PLACEMENT DECISION

5.22 The Act lays down a number of principles which should guide the local authority's choice of placement of a child, while more detailed duties will be found in regulations. The welfare duty, religious, racial, cultural and linguistic considerations and requirements of consultation will apply (*paragraphs 5.9–5.12*), but section 23 adds four further duties:

(a) Arrangements should be made to enable a child to live with a person connected with the child unless that would not be reasonably practicable or consistent with his welfare [*section 23(6)*]. Examples of persons 'connected' are a child's parent, any other person with parental responsibility for him or, where a child is in care, a person who had the benefit of a residence order immediately before the care order was made, a relative or a friend of the child. Regulations may be made regarding this duty.

(b) So far as is reasonably practicable and consistent with the child's welfare, accommodation should be provided which is near to the child's home [*section 23(7)(a)*].

(c) So far as is reasonably practicable and consistent with the child's welfare, where accommodation is provided for siblings, they should be accommodated together [*section 23(7)(b)*].

(d) Where a child is disabled, so far as is reasonably practicable, accommodation should not be unsuitable to his needs [*section 23(8)*].

5.23 A local authority may arrange (or assist in arranging) for a child whom they are looking after to live outside England and Wales with the approval of every person who has parental responsibility for the child [*Schedule 2, paragraph 19(2)*]. In the case of a child who is in care, the court's approval must be sought [*Schedule 2, paragraph 19(1)*]. This may only be given in certain circumstances, namely where: every person with parental responsibility for the child consents or his consent is dispensed with under paragraph 19(5), the child himself consents (if he has sufficient understanding), suitable arrangements have been made for the reception and welfare of the child in the new country and living there would be in the child's best interests [*Schedule 2, paragraph 19(3) and (4)*]. Where the child is moving to another jurisdiction within the British Islands the court may be able to transfer the effect of the care order to the relevant public authority in the receiving jurisdiction [*under regulations made by virtue of section 101*].

5.24 The use of secure accommodation by local authorities is subject to restrictions similar to those which applied under the Child Care Act 1980. Any child who is looked after by a local authority may only be placed in secure accommodation if:

(a) (i) he has a history of absconding and is likely to abscond from any other description of accommodation; and

(ii) if he absconds, he is likely to suffer harm; or

(b) that if he is kept in any other description of accommodation he is likely to injure himself or other persons.

Regulations will set the maximum period beyond which secure accommodation may not be used without authorisation by a court [*section 25(2). These regulations will replace the Secure Accommodation (No. 2) Regulations 1983 and the Secure Accommodation (No. 2) (Amendment) Regulations 1986*]. A child who is accommodated under section 20 may be removed from accommodation by a person with parental responsibility for him even if that accommodation is secure and a secure order has been granted [*section 25(9)*].

CONTACT

5.25 The Children Act imposes a new duty to promote contact between a child who is being looked after and those who are connected with him [*Schedule 2, paragraph 15(1). These people include the child's parents, any one else with parental responsibility for him and any relative or friend of the child*] unless it is not reasonably practicable or consistent with the child's welfare to do so. Contact embraces more than face-to-face visits and sometimes it will be more appropriate to promote contact by letter or telephone rather than by visit. To support the new duty, the local authority are required to take reasonable steps to inform the child's parents and any other person who has parental responsibility for the child of the child's address [*Schedule 2, paragraph 15(2).*]. However, information need not be given if the child is under a care order and it would prejudice the child's welfare to give it [*Schedule 2, paragraph 15(4)*]. A parent or other person with parental responsibility for the child must inform the local authority of his address, [*Schedule 2, paragraph 15(2)(b).*]. The local authority may also make payments to assist visits between the child and a person connected with him, if the visits would otherwise cause undue financial hardship and the circumstances warrant the payment [*Schedule 2, paragraph 16. These payments may be for travel, subsistence and other expenses*].

5.26 Where a child is in care the local authority must allow reasonable contact with a child's parents, any guardian and any other person with whom he was living under a court order immediately before the care order was made [*section 34(1). The court order may be a residence order or an order under the inherent jurisdiction of the High Court*]. The power to withhold contact in an emergency and for the court to make orders regarding contact were set out in Chapter 3 (*paragraphs 3.65–3.69*). In the unlikely event of a contact dispute when a child is *not* in care a section 7 order could be made on the application of the child, a parent or other person, (*paragraphs 3.46 and 3.47.*). Regulations will require local authorities to notify those affected of proposals to change arrangements for contact. If those arrangements are defined in a court order the regulations may provide for the terms of the order to be departed from with the agreement of the person named in the order [*section 34(8)*].

5.27 Where it would be in a child's best interests, an independent visitor must be appointed for him, if he has not stayed with or been visited by a parent of his or a person who has parental responsibility for him for a period of twelve months, or communication between the child and such a person has been infrequent [*Schedule 2, paragraph 17(1)*]. Under the old law the appointment of visitors was restricted to children who were accommodated in community homes which provided education [*section 11 of the Child Care Act 1980.*]. An independent visitor (who may be a relative or friend of the child, but must be independent of the authority) will visit, advise and befriend the child [*Schedule 2, paragraph 17(2). The visitor is entitled to recover his reasonable expenses*]. An appointment may not be made, or if made should be terminated, if the child objects to it and is of sufficient understanding to make an informed decision [*Schedule 2, paragraphs 17(5) and (6).*]. An independent visitor may, of course, resign and another appointment may have to be made [*Schedule 2, paragraph 17(3)*].

REVIEWS

5.28 The duty to plan for and review the case of each child who is looked after will be dealt with comprehensively in regulations [*section 26(1) and (2)*]. Regulations will cover the frequency and manner of reviews, as well as the duty to involve the child and his parents (and others whose views are relevant) in the review process. In the case of a child who is in care, the review will have to consider whether the care order should be discharged. If a child is accommodated under section 20 and it would not be in the child's interests for him to return home, the review will need to address whether steps should be taken to prevent this, for example by applying for a care order or, if the child is living with foster parents, by their applying for a residence order.

EDUCATION

5.29 Where the authority which look after a child propose to place him in an establishment at which education is provided for children who live there, they must consult the local education authority first, so far as is reasonably practicable [*section 28(1)*]. If the child has a special educational needs statement, the local education authority who maintain the statement should be consulted. Otherwise, it is the education authority for the area which the local authority serve [*section 28(4)*]. They must also inform the local education authority as soon as is reasonably practicable if the child does go to live there and, if so, when he leaves [*section 28(2) and (3)*].

REPRESENTATIONS AND COMPLAINTS

5.30 The procedure which was discussed in Chapter 4 will be available to consider representations about the exercise of local authority responsibilities in respect of children whom they are looking after (*paragraphs 4.32–4.34*). When a child is in care a section 8 order will not be available in respect of him, other than a residence order which discharges the care order (*paragraph 3.46*). However, the Act does not prevent applications being made for section 8 orders in respect of other children who are being looked after (subject to the general requirements regarding the leave of the court).

CONTRIBUTIONS TO MAINTENANCE

5.31 A local authority which is looking after a child must consider whether or not to recover contributions towards the cost of the child's maintenance from a parent of the child or, when he is sixteen, the child himself. The only exceptions to this are where a child is looked after under an interim care order, an emergency protection order (or any other provision of Part V) or certain other criminal provisions [*Schedule 2, paragraph 21*]. Contributions may only be recovered when the authority considers it reasonable to do so and not at all from a parent who is in receipt of income support or family credit or while the child is allowed to live with a parent of his. [*Schedule 2, paragraph 21(2)–(4)*].

5.32 The procedure for recovery of contributions has been simplified since the Child Care Act 1980. The local authority which want to receive contributions must serve a contribution notice on the contributor, specifying a weekly sum which is not greater than that which they would be prepared to pay foster parents for looking after a similar child and which it is reasonable to expect the contributor to pay. The notice must also state the proposed arrangements for payment [*Schedule 2, paragraph 22*]. If the contributor does not agree with the sum and arrangements for payment (as specified in the notice or otherwise proposed by the authority), or if he withdraws his agreement, the authority may apply to court for a contribution order. This order may not specify a sum greater than that which was in the contribution notice. If the contributor and the local authority agree the terms of a new contribution notice, this agreement will discharge an existing contribution order. Failing agreement, a contribution order may be varied or discharged on the application of the contributor or the local authority [*Schedule 2, paragraph 23*].

AFTER-CARE: WHEN A CHILD CEASES TO BE LOOKED AFTER

5.33 Local authorities are required to advise, assist and befriend each child whom they look after with a view to promoting his welfare when he ceases to be looked after by them [*section 24(1)*]. Steps should be taken to prepare a child for the time when he is no longer looked after.

5.34 A person 'qualifies for advice and assistance' when he ceases to be looked after. 'A person qualifying for advice and assistance' means a person within the area of the authority who is under 21 and who was, at any time after reaching the age of 16 but while still a child:

(a) looked after by a local authority;

(b) accommodated by or on behalf of a voluntary organisation;

(c) accommodated in a registered children's home;

(d) accommodated–

(i) by any health authority or local education authority; or

(ii) in any residential care home, nursing home or mental nursing home, for a consecutive period of at least three months; or

(e) privately fostered,

but who is no longer so looked after, accommodated or fostered. In the case of (a) and (b) above local authorities are *required* to advise and befriend a person who qualifies for advice and assistance in their area (and are *empowered* to do so in the case of (c) to (e) above) if:

(i) it appears that the person needs advice and to be befriended;

(ii) he asks the authority for help of a kind which they can give to those who qualify for advice and assistance [*section 24(4) and (5)*].

5.35 The Authorities are also *empowered* to assist any person in (a) to (e) above who qualifies, by providing assistance in kind and, in exceptional circumstances, in cash [*section 24(6) and (7)*]. Assistance may be made subject to conditions as to whole or partial repayment. Before giving assistance or imposing conditions, an authority must have regard to the means of the child and of each of his parents. A person is not liable to repay at any time while he is in receipt of income support or family credit [*section 24(10), which applies section 17(7)–(9)*].

5.36 Assistance may include making a grant to enable the person who qualifies to meet expenses connected with his education and training or contributing to expenses incurred by him in living near the place where he is or will be employed, seeking employment or receiving education or training [*section 24(8)*]. In such cases the 'exceptional circumstances' qualification to cash assistance does not apply [*section 21(7)*]; nor can repayment of assistance be required [*section 24(10)*]. The grant or contribution may continue beyond the person's twenty-first birthday to help him complete the course [*section 24(9)*].

5.37 If a 'qualified' person is being advised and befriended and he goes to live (or proposes to go to live) in the area of another local authority, the local authority which is advising and befriending him must inform the new local authority [*section 24(12)*].

DEATH OF A CHILD WHO IS BEING LOOKED AFTER

5.38 If a child who is being looked after dies, the local authority must notify the Secretary of State and, so far as is reasonably practicable, the child's parents and any other person who has parental responsibility for him [*Schedule 2, paragraph 20(1)*]. The authority may also arrange for the burial of the child (or his cremation, unless it does not accord with the child's religious persuasion) with the consent of each person who has parental responsibility for the child, so far as it is reasonably practicable to obtain it [*Schedule 2, paragraph 20(1)(c) and (3)*]. If the child was under sixteen when he died, the expenses relating to burial or cremation may be recovered from a parent of the child [*Schedule 2, paragraph 20(4)*].

5.39 Travelling, subsistence or other expenses incurred by any person connected with the child in attending the child's funeral may be paid by the authority if that person could not otherwise attend without undue financial hardship and the circumstances warrant payment [*Schedule 2, paragraph 20(1)(d) and (2). A person connected with the child includes persons with parental responsibility for him, his relatives and friends.*].

TRANSITIONAL PROVISIONS

5.40 Where a child was in voluntary care at the time Part III of the Act came into force, he is treated as provided with accommodation under section 20 of the Act. In line with the principles in Part III, if such a child had been placed with a parent, guardian or a person who had care and control of the child under a court order, he is not treated as provided with accommodation [*Schedule 14, paragraph 20*]. Under the old law it was not clear whether 'voluntary care' continued in these circumstances. (For the effect of old-style care orders and parental rights resolutions which were in force when the Act was implemented see paragraphs 3.125–3.132).

5.41 Placements under the old law of a child in compulsory care with a parent, guardian or a person who had the right to care and control of the child under a court order are in future treated as Accommodation of Children placements under the regulations which replace the (Charge and Control) Regulations 1988 [*Schedule 14, paragraph 17*]. Other family placements are treated as if they had been made under the regulations which will replace the Boarding-out (Foster Placement) Regulations 1988 [*Schedule 14, paragraph 21*]. However, to allow a period of adjustment, the new fostering regulations will not apply for twelve months. Meanwhile, the existing regulations will continue to apply (i.e. the Charge and Control or Foster Placement Regulations, as appropriate). The result is that the old Charge and Control Regulations continue to apply to placements of children with relatives and friends even if they do not have an order in their favour for care and control of the child.

5.42 Children who left care under the old law when they were 16 or 17 and are now under 21 qualify for advice and assistance from the local authority in whose area they are (*after care is subject to the rules in paragraphs 5.33–5.37*). [*Schedule 14, paragraph 22*].

5.43 Orders under the old law requiring contributions to be made to a local authority for a child in care are treated as if they had been made under the Act [*Schedule 14, paragraph 24*].

CHAPTER 6 <u>PROTECTION OF CHILDREN AT RISK</u>

6.1 This chapter describes the investigative duties of local authorities and the measures which are available to local authorities and others under Part V of the Act to protect children. Three new orders are created by the Act: an emergency protection order, a child assessment order and a recovery order. The police may take children who are at risk into 'police protection' and warrants are available to enter specified premises to search for children.

6.2 The provisions explained in this chapter replace the investigative duties in the Children and Young Persons Act 1969 [*section 2 of that Act*]. Also repealed are the numerous powers to take children to places of safety, in particular 'the place of safety order' under section 28 of the 1969 Act. This order, which could be made on an *ex parte* application to a magistrate without evidence that the child was at immediate risk, enabled a child to be removed for as long as 28 days with no right of appeal or challenge. Additionally, the powers and duties of the person who obtained the place of safety order were uncertain. These aspects of the order have been justifiably criticised and the Children Act tries to find a better balance between the need to protect children and the other interests of the individuals involved. The conditions which must be satisfied before an emergency protection or child assessment order may be made are closely linked to the purpose of these orders; where practicable parents and others are given a right of challenge; the duration of the orders is shorter than the place of safety order; and the legal effect of both of these orders is more clearly spelt out.

INVESTIGATION BY LOCAL AUTHORITIES

6.3 A local authority is under an investigative duty in five circumstances:

(a) where they have reasonable cause to suspect that a child who lives or is found in their area is suffering or is likely to suffer significant harm [*section 47(1)(b)*];

(b) where they have obtained an emergency protection order in respect of a child [*section 47(2)*];

(c) where they are informed that a child who lives or is found in their area is subject to an emergency protection order or is in police protection [*section 47(1) (a)*].

(d) where a court in family proceedings directs them to investigate a child's circumstances [*section 37(1) and on the discharge of an education supervision order: paragraph 17(2) of Schedule 3*]

(e) where a local education authority notify them that a child is persistently failing to comply with directions given under an education supervision order [*paragraph 19 of Schedule 3*];

6.4 With the exception of (d) and (e) which were described in Chapter 3 (*paragraphs 3.106–3.107*), the investigative duty is the same: namely, to make or cause to be made (for example by another agency such as the NSPCC) such inquiries as they consider necessary to enable them to decide whether they should take any action to safeguard or promote the child's welfare [*section 47(1) and (2)*]. Even where the authority carry out inquiries through another agency, it is up to the authority themselves to decide whether to take any action with respect to the child. If an authority are carrying out an investigation they may call upon another agency to assist them, for example by providing information and advice. Certain agencies (another local authority, a local education authority, a local housing authority, a health authority or any other person who is authorised by the Secretary of State) are required to assist the local authority unless it would be unreasonable for them to have to do so [*section 47(9) and (11)*].

6.5 In particular, the aim of an inquiry should be to establish whether the authority need to exercise any of their powers under the Act with respect to the child [*section 47(3)*]. They may decide that an application should be made to a court, for example for a care or supervision order, or they may decide to offer services to the child or his family under Part III of the Act (*Chapter 4*). Where a child may be at risk of ill-treatment at the hands of another person who is living on the same premises, the authority may decide to take steps other than the removal of the child. The Act makes specific mention of assistance (including cash) which may be provided to the person whom it is feared may ill-treat the child, so that he may find alternative accommodation [*Schedule 2, paragraph 5*]. Alternatively, the authority may advise and assist that person's spouse or cohabitee to apply for an order excluding him from their home. If the authority conclude that action, which they have power to take, should be taken in the child's interests, they are required to take this action if it is reasonably practicable for them to do so [*section 47(8)*].

6.6 When carrying out the investigative duty, the local authority should try to see the child so that they can properly decide whether they should take any action for his benefit. Unless they are satisfied that they already have sufficient information about the child (for example because they are already familiar with his present circumstances), they are required to take steps which are reasonably practicable either to obtain access to the child themselves or to ensure that access to him is obtained on their behalf by someone who is authorised by them for the purpose [*section 47(4)*]. This latter person might be an officer of the NSPCC or a doctor.

6.7 If an officer of the authority or a person authorised to act on their behalf is refused access to the child concerned or denied information about his whereabouts the authority must apply for an order to protect the child unless they are satisfied that his welfare can be satisfactorily safeguarded by other means [*section 47(6)*]. The most common orders sought will be an emergency protection order, a child assessment order or a care or supervision order.

6.8 Several other specific duties may arise while a local authority is carrying out an investigation. These are as follows:

(a) if a child has been made subject to an emergency protection order, and he is not in accommodation which is provided by the local authority, the local authority must direct their inquiries towards establishing whether the child should be in such accommodation while the order is in force [*section 47(3)(b)*];

(b) where a child has been taken into police protection, the local authority are also required to direct their inquiries towards establishing whether they should ask the police to apply on their behalf for an emergency protection order [*section 47(3)(c)*], (*see paragraph 6.35 below*);

(c) if the authority decide that there are matters relating to the child's education which need to be investigated, they should consult the local education authority [*section 47(5)*];

(d) where the authority are investigating the circumstances of a child who usually lives in the area of another local authority, they must consult that other authority who may undertake the necessary inquiries in their area [*section 47(12)*].

6.9 If the local authority decide not to apply for an emergency protection, child assessment, care or supervision order, they must consider whether they should review the child's case later [*section 47(7)*]. If they decide to hold a review, they must fix the date on which it is to begin.

EMERGENCY PROTECTION ORDERS

6.10 An emergency protection order is a short term order which enables a child to be made safe when he might otherwise suffer harm. It may be applied for by anyone but may only be made in one of the following circumstances:

(a) the court is satisfied that there is reasonable cause to believe that the child is likely to suffer significant harm if either:

> (i) he is not removed to accommodation provided by or on behalf of the applicant; or

> (ii) he does not remain in the place in which he is then being accommodated [*section 44(1)(a)*];

6.11 Condition (a) may be relied upon by any person who is seeking an emergency protection order. It requires that the court (and not just the applicant) is satisfied that there is reasonable cause to believe that the child is likely to suffer significant harm. The test is entirely prospective: evidence of harm which occurred in the past is not sufficient unless it indicates that further harm is more likely than not to occur. 'Significant harm' has the same meaning as it has in the conditions for a care or supervision order: it includes ill-treatment as well as impairment of health or development (*paragraphs 3.52–3.54*). An order may be sought either to remove a child *or* to detain him. The latter would cover the child who is already in hospital and who is likely to suffer if he is allowed to return home.

(b) where the court is satisfied on the application of a local authority that:

> (i) the local authority is carrying out an investigation under their statutory duty described in paragraph 6.3(a) above (because they have reasonable cause to suspect that a child who lives or is found in their area is suffering or is likely to suffer significant harm);

> (ii) the authority's inquiries are being frustrated by access to the child being unreasonably refused to an officer of the authority or a person authorised by the authority to act on their behalf in connection with the inquiries; and

> (iii) the authority has reasonable cause to believe that access to the child is required as a matter of urgency [*section 44(1)(b)*].

6.12 Condition (b) may only be relied upon by a local authority applicant carrying out a statutory investigation under the duty described above. Under that duty, the authority is required to obtain access to the child unless it already has sufficient information with respect to the child. Where access to the child or information as to his whereabouts is refused, they must consider whether to apply for a court order. Condition (b) is designed with these circumstances in mind. An emergency protection order may only be made if the court finds that the local authority's inquiries are being frustrated by an unreasonable refusal of access to the child and that the applicant reasonably believes that access is required as a matter of urgency.

6.13 In most, if not all, applications under condition (b) the court will make its decision on the evidence provided by the local authority alone, since it will not have been appropriate and practicable to serve notice of the application on the person caring for the child. To discover whether there has been an unreasonable refusal of access, the court will need to know what efforts have been made to see the child and what responses have been made by the child's carers. Where a call is made when the child is asleep, it *may* be reasonable for a parent to refuse to disturb the child and to offer to take the child to a local clinic or nursery later in the day or the following morning. Such an offer may not be an unreasonable refusal of access where the risk to a child is believed to be immediate or where previous arrangements have been broken. Where a person is seeking access to a child, they must produce evidence of their authority if asked to do so [*section 44(3)*]. Failure to produce such evidence may make a refusal of access reasonable.

(c) where the court is satisfied on the application of a person who is authorised by the Secretary of State to apply for care and supervision orders (the NSPCC and its officers) that:

> (i) the authorised person who is making the application has reasonable cause to suspect that a child is suffering or is likely to suffer significant harm;

> (ii) the authorised person is making inquiries with respect to the child's welfare;

> (iii) those inquiries are being frustrated by an unreasonable refusal of access to the authorised person; and

> (iv) the authorised person has reasonable cause to believe that access to the child is required as a matter of urgency [*section 44(1)(c)*].

6.14 Condition (c) is the same as (b) except that it may only be used by the authorised person who is carrying out inquiries into the child's welfare. It recognises that, although they are not under a statutory duty to investigate children at risk, the NSPCC play an important role in investigation alongside local authorities. Where they carry out inquiries into cases of suspected harm, they should be given the same powers as those authorities to protect the children involved.

6.15 Even where one of the above conditions is satisfied, the court will not automatically make an emergency order. It is required to apply the principles set out in Chapter 3: in particular, the welfare principle (although the checklist in section 1(2) does not have to be applied) and the presumption of no order (*paragraphs 3.13–3.25*).

The Effect of Emergency Protection Orders

6.16 An emergency protection order requires any person who is in a position to do so to produce the child to the applicant [*section 44(4) (a)*]. It also authorises either the removal of the child to accommodation provided by or on behalf of the applicant (and his being kept there) or the prevention of the child's removal from a hospital or other place in which he was being accommodated when the order was made [*section 44(4)(b). It may be an offence to obstruct these powers: section 44(15)*]. When the applicant has an order in his favour he may only remove the child, or prevent his removal, in order to safeguard the child's welfare [*section 44(5)(a)*].

If, for example, an order is obtained to get access to a child and, when the child is found, it turns out that the child is safe in his home, the applicant cannot remove him.

6.17 Similarly, where a child has been removed under an emergency protection order, or his removal has been prevented, the applicant must return the child, or allow him to be removed (as appropriate), if it would be safe to do so [*section 44(10)*]. If the child has been removed (and it is safe) he should be returned to the care of the person from whose care he was removed. If that is not reasonably practicable, the child should be returned to the care of a parent of his or of another person with parental responsibility for him. Alternatively, the child may be returned to the care of another appropriate person, provided the applicant has obtained the agreement of the court [*section 44(11)*]. Even where a child has been returned, or allowed to be removed, because it appeared to be safe, the emergency order remains in force and the applicant may again exercise his powers with respect to the child (for example to remove the child) if a change in circumstances makes it necessary [*section 44(12)*].

6.18 The applicant is given parental responsibility for the child [*section 44(4)(c)*]. He is required to take, but to only take, such action in meeting his parental responsibility as is reasonably required to safeguard or promote the welfare of the child (bearing in mind the duration of the order) [*section 44(5)(b)*]. He may not, for example, arrange for the child to move to a new school, although, if appropriate, he may make temporary arrangements for the child's education while the order lasts. Regulations may be made to impose further requirements on the applicant [*section 44(5)(c)*].

6.19 The applicant must allow the child reasonable contact with his parents, any other person who has parental responsibility for him, the person with whom he was living immediately before the order was made, any person in whose favour an order relating to contact is in force with respect to him (whether it is a section 8 'contact order' or was made under section 34 of the Act) and any person acting on behalf of those persons (such as a doctor or an independent social worker) [*section 44(13)*]. Subject to the court's directions, it is for the applicant to decide what constitutes reasonable contact. It may only be reasonable to allow a person suspected of abuse to have contact which is under supervision.

The Court's Powers

6.20 Where it makes an emergency protection order, or at any time thereafter while the order is in force, the court may make directions as to the contact which is or is not to be allowed between the child and any named person [*section 44(6)*]. It may decide that a person who is suspected of abuse of the child should lose their right to reasonable contact. Or a person's contact might be restricted by certain conditions (for example as to the time or place of a visit) [*section 44(6)*]. Directions as to contact may be varied on the application of those who are specified in rules of court [*section 44(9)*].

6.21 The court has a similar power to make and to vary directions as to the medical or psychiatric examination or other assessment of the child while an emergency protection order is in force [*section 44(6) and (9)*]. A direction may also provide that there should be no such examination or assessment (or not unless the court directs otherwise) [*section 44(8)*]. These powers are the same as those which arise when a child is in interim care or under interim supervision (*paragraphs 3.58–3.64*). Just as in those cases, a child who is of sufficient understanding to make an informed decision may refuse to submit to an examination or other assessment, even if a court has directed that it should take place [*section 44(7)*].

6.22 When it makes an emergency order, the court may make additional directions or orders which may assist the applicant. These are as follows:

(a) it may direct that the applicant may be accompanied by a registered medical practitioner, registered nurse or registered health visitor, if he so chooses, when he exercises any of his powers under the order [*section 45(12)*]. The presence of such a professional may enable the applicant to decide whether he needs to remove a child;

(b) if adequate information as to the child's whereabouts is not available to the applicant but seems to be available to another person, the court may require that other person to disclose the information which he has to the applicant [*section 48(1)*]. The person asked cannot refuse to give that information on the ground that his answer may incriminate himself or his spouse but his answer will not be used against either him or his spouse in later criminal proceedings except perjury [*section 48(2)*]. (*See also paragraph 8.23*).

(c) the court may authorise the applicant to enter specified premises and to search for the child concerned [*section 48(3)*]. Obstruction of this power may be an offence [*section 48(7)*]. (*For the police's powers of entry see paragraph 6.30 below*);

(d) it may also authorise the applicant to search for another child who there is reasonable cause to believe may be on the same premises and ought also to be under an emergency protection order [*section 48(4)*. Obstruction of this power may also be an offence: *section 48(7)*]. This power is intended to secure that, where an emergency protection order has been obtained in respect of one child, search may be authorised for other children who may also need to be protected. If another such child is found on the premises and the applicant is satisfied that the grounds for making an emergency protection order exist with respect to him, the court's authorisation of the search has the effect of an emergency protection order, enabling that child to be removed [*section 48(5)*]. Where the court makes an authorisation under (d) the applicant must notify the court of its effect [*section 48(6)*];

(e) a warrant may be issued to a constable to assist (using reasonable force if necessary) a person who has been, or is likely to be, prevented from exercising powers under an emergency protection order by being refused entry to the premises concerned or access to the child concerned [*section 48(9)*]. The warrant must be addressed to a constable who may be accompanied in the execution of the warrant by the person who applied for it, unless the court directs otherwise [*section 48(10)*]. The court may also direct that the constable may be accompanied by a registered medical practitioner, registered nurse or registered health visitor, if he so chooses [*section 48(11)*].

Duration of Emergency Protection Orders

6.23 An emergency protection order will have effect for as long as the court specifies, subject to a maximum of eight days [*section 45(1)*]. If the eighth day is a public holiday, the court may specify a period which ends at noon on the first day after the holiday [*section*

45(2)]. A local authority or authorised person who has parental responsibility for a child under an emergency order may ask a court to extend the effect of the order for a period of up to seven days [*section 45(4) and (5)*]. An extension would enable either of them to have more time in which to prepare to make an application for a care or supervision order. However, the original emergency protection order should normally give them sufficient time to do this. If an extension is sought, rules of court will require the applicant to give the court his reasons for not being ready to apply for care or supervision, if that is the reason for an extension being needed. An order may only be extended once and may not be extended unless the court has reasonable cause to believe that the child concerned is likely to suffer significant harm in the absence of an extension [*section 45(5) and (6)*].

6.24 Most emergency protection orders will be made without the court having heard more than the applicant's side of the story. It might put the child concerned at greater risk if prior notice of an application had to be served on his carer or if there was an immediate right of challenge to the order. However, the Act gives the child, a parent of his, any other person with parental responsibility for him and any other person with whom he was living immediately before the order was made, the right to apply for the discharge of an emergency protection order [*section 45(8)*]. Such an application can only be heard at least 72 hours after the order was made [*section 45(9)*]. In the rare case of a person having been given notice of the original application for the emergency order and being present at the hearing at which the order was made, that person will not be entitled to apply for discharge of the order [*section 45(11)*]. Also, an order which has been extended may not be discharged, since those interested will have been given a chance to oppose the making of the extension [*section 45(10). Extension hearings will be on notice*].

Court Procedure

6.25 Rules of Court will set out the form in which applications should be made and directions should be given [*section 52*]. The Act requires that an emergency protection order, an order authorising a search for a child who ought to be under an emergency protection order, an application for a warrant and the warrant itself should name the child concerned or describe him as closely as possible [*sections 44(14) and 48(13)*]. Rules of Court will also provide for the notification of people about applications and orders relating to emergency protection.

6.26 As was mentioned in Chapter 3, a guardian *ad litem* may be appointed to protect the child's interests when an application is made under Part V of the Act (*paragraph 3.114*). The guardian might, for example, be able to assist a child who wished to apply to court in respect of the emergency order or regarding directions which may be made under it. He also might be able to advise the court about the discharge of the emergency order, its extension and directions which may be made. Where a court is hearing an application for or relating to an emergency protection order, it may take account of a statement contained in a report made to the court or any evidence given during the hearing even if the hearsay rule, or another rule of evidence, or an enactment would otherwise prevent it from doing so [*section 45(7)*].

6.27 Unlike most other decisions under the Act, no appeal may be made against the making or refusal to make an emergency protection order or against any direction given by the court in connection with the order [*section 45(10)*].

6.28 Where a child who lives or is found in their area is subject to an emergency protection order, a local authority are under a duty to investigate his circumstances [*section 47(1)*]. The same duty arises where the authority obtain an emergency protection order [*section 47(2)*]. In particular, they should establish whether he ought to be in accommodation which is provided by them or on their behalf, as well as whether they should exercise any of their powers under the Act with respect to him [*section 47(3)*]. Where the child is accommodated by or on behalf of the local authority, he is 'looked after' by the authority and the provisions explained in Chapter 5 apply.

6.29 Regulations will provide for the local authority in whose area a child usually lives to take over the reponsibility for a child who is subject to an emergency protection order [*section 52(3)*]. Where that authority consider that it would be in the best interests of the child for this to happen, the authority will be treated as if they were the applicant for the emergency order, instead of the person who had originally applied. The local authority will then have parental responsibility for the child and will take the decisions about where the child will be accommodated and whether an application should be made for the order to be extended. Before such transfer of responsibility may take place, the authority will have to observe the requirements of the regulations, such as regarding consultation with the original applicant and, where that person is the NSPCC, obtaining their consent to the transfer.

POLICE PROTECTION

6.30 The power of a constable to take a child to a place of safety (without obtaining a court order) is replaced by the power to take the child into police protection. This power may be exercised where the constable has reasonable cause to believe that a child would otherwise be likely to suffer significant harm [*section 46(1)*]. It is exercised by the constable either:

(a) removing the child to suitable accommodation and keeping him there; or

(b) taking reasonable steps to ensure that the child's removal from a hospital, or other place, in which he is being accommodated is prevented [*under the Police and Criminal Evidence Act 1984, the police may enter and search premises "to save life and limb", section 17(i)(e)*].

6.31 Police protection cannot last for longer than 72 hours [*section 46(6)*]. As soon as is reasonably practicable after taking a child into police protection, the constable must secure that the case is inquired into by an officer who has been designated for this purpose [*section 46(3)(e). Designation is by the chief officer of the police area concerned.*]. That officer must release the child when his inquiry is completed unless he considers that there is still reasonable cause to believe that the child would be likely to suffer significant harm if released [*section 46(5)*].

6.32 While a child is in police protection the designated officer must do what is reasonable in all the circumstances to safeguard or promote the child's welfare, bearing in mind the length of time police protection will last [*section 46(9)*]. He does not have parental responsibility for the child.

6.33 Apart from initiating an inquiry, the constable must do the following things (as soon as is reasonably practicable):

(a) inform the child (if he is capable of understanding) of what steps have been taken with respect to him regarding his being in police protection, the reasons for taking them and what further steps may be taken [*section 46(3)(c)*];

(b) take steps which are reasonably practicable to discover the child's wishes and feelings [*section 46(3)(d)*];

(c) inform the child's parents, and any other person who has parental responsibility for him or with whom he was living when he was taken into police protection, of the matters referred to in [*section 46(4)*];

(d) inform the local authority within whose area the child was found of the matters referred to in [*section 46(3)(a)*];

(e) inform the local authority for the area in which the child usually lives of the place at which he is being accommodated [*section 46(3)(b)*];

(f) where the child is not in accommodation provided by or on behalf of a local authority, or provided by a refuge, secure that he is moved to accommodation which is so provided [*section 46(3)(f)*]. (*For refuges, see paragraph 6.53 below*).

6.34 While the child is in police protection, the designated officer must allow such contact with the child (if any) which is reasonable and in the child's best interests, to the child's parents, anyone else who has got parental responsibility for him or with whom the child was living when he was taken into police protection, a person who has in his favour an order relating to contact, or any person acting on behalf of any of the above [*section 46(10). The order relating to contact may be a section 8 order or an order made under section 34.*] If the child in police protection is accommodated by the local authority for the area in which the child usually lives, the authority is required to afford such contact to these people [*section 46(11)*].

6.35 Where a child continues to need protection, the intention is that a local authority should take up the reins while he is still in police protection. The child should have been accommodated with an authority and duties of investigation fall upon that authority, as well as the authority for the area where the child usually lives, if different [*section 47(1)*]. In the unusual case in which the local authority are not ready to act, or where the police disagree with the decision of the local authority not to obtain a court order to protect the child, the designated officer may apply for an emergency protection order on behalf of the local authority for the area in which the child usually lives [*section 46(7) and (8)*]. That local authority must then carry out the responsibilities of the emergency order. One of the local authority's investigative duties when a child is in police protection is to discover whether they should ask the police to apply for an emergency protection order on their behalf [*section 47(3)(c)*].

CHILD ASSESSMENT ORDERS

6.36 A child assessment order may be made on the application of a local authority or a person who is authorised to apply for a care or supervision order (namely, the NSPCC and its officers). It may only be made where the court is satisfied that:

"(a) the applicant has reasonable cause to suspect that the child is suffering, or is likely to suffer, significant harm;

(b) an assessment of the state of the child's health or development, or of the way in which he has been treated, is required to enable the applicant to determine whether or not the child is suffering, or is likely to suffer, significant harm; and

(c) it is unlikely that such an assessment will be made, or be satisfactory, in the absence of an order under this section."
[*section 43(1)*]

Where these conditions are satisfied, the court will decide whether to make an order applying the welfare principle and the presumption of no order (*paragraphs 3.14–3.25*). However, it should also consider whether the more appropriate order in the circumstances is an emergency protection order, in which case the application should be treated as an application for such an order and a child assessment order should not be made [*section 43(3) and (4)*]. The question of which order is more appropriate is considered below after the effect of an assessment order has been explained.

6.37 The Act does not restrict the type of assessment which may be carried out under a child assessment order. Each order authorises the person carrying out the assessment to do so in accordance with its terms [*section 43(7)*]. An order must specify the date on which the assessment is to begin and the order will have effect for a maximum of seven days from that date [*section 43(5)*]. The order may also contain terms which:

(a) specify the person to whom the child is to be produced by any person who is a position to do so;

(b) limit the duration of the order to less than seven days;

(c) make directions on any matter relating to the assessment [*section 43(5) and (6)*].

6.38 Category (c) may include directions as to what kind of assessment is to take place and with what aim, by whom and where it will be carried out and whether it will be subject to conditions, such as that the assessment should be a joint one involving experts appointed by the child's parents or guardian *ad litem* as well as by the local authority. If the child is to be kept away from home during an assessment, the order must make directions authorising this [*section 43(9)*]. If the court so directs, the order must also contain directions as to the contact which is to be allowed with other people while he is away from home [*section 43(10)*]. The child may only be kept away from home as specified in the order and if it is necessary to do so for the purposes of the assessment [*section 43(9)*].

6.39 A child assessment order does not authorise an assessment or examination which the child refuses to undergo (provided that he is of sufficient understanding to make an informed decision about this question) [*section 43(8)*]. The court may appoint a guardian *ad litem* to protect the interests of the child in proceedings relating to child assessment orders [*section 41(6)(g)*]. The duties of the guardian were described in Chapter 3 (*paragraphs 3.112–3.116*). In this context the guardian may be able to provide the court with independent advice as to the need for and details of an assessment.

6.40 The applicant for a child assessment order must take steps which are reasonably practicable to ensure that prior notice of the application is given to the child, his parents, any other person who has parental responsibility for the child or with whom the child is living and a person in whose favour an order relating to contact is in force with respect to the child [*whether the contact order is a section 8 order or was made under section 34: section 43(11)*]. Rules of court will provide for the circumstances in which, and on the application of whom, a child assessment order may be varied or discharged [*section 43(12)*]. A further application for a child assessment order may not be made (without the leave of the court) within six months of the disposal of the previous one or the disposal of an application for the discharge of a care or supervision order etc. [*section 91(15)*] (*see paragraphs 3.110–3.111*).

The Purpose of the Order

6.41 The child assessment order is a new order which provides for cases in which there is reasonable concern about the child, the people caring for him are uncooperative, but there is no case to warrant an application for either an emergency protection order or a care or supervision order. The conditions for a child assessment order indicate that, like the emergency protection order, it is available to assist a local authority which is carrying out its investigative duty with respect to a child. It is also available to an authorised person who is inquiring into the circumstances of a child. Therefore, the first condition for both orders requires that the applicant has reasonable cause to suspect that the child is suffering or is likely to suffer significant harm. Both orders also enable the court to make directions regarding the assessment of the child. However, the second two conditions indicate that the purpose of the child assessment order is quite different from the emergency protection order.

6.42 The child assessment order may be made where it is otherwise unlikely that a satisfactory assessment of the child's health or development, or of the way in which he has been treated, will be obtained and where, without an assessment, the applicant cannot find out whether the child is suffering or likely to suffer significant harm. In short, the applicant's attempts to achieve an **assessment** have been frustrated. The child may well have been seen, to rule out the need for an emergency protection order.

6.43 Where an emergency protection order is needed the child's circumstances may well be as described in the previous paragraph. However, there is also a more immediate risk to the child: either the applicant knows enough to persuade the court that there is reasonable cause to believe that the child is likely to suffer if action is not taken to protect him *or* the applicant reasonably suspects that access to the child is required as a matter of urgency but access has been unreasonably refused. In the latter case it is **access** which is needed to confirm that the child is safe, but the applicant's attempts to obtain it have been frustrated.

6.44 The differences between the orders are reflected in other provisions of the Act. Child assessment orders are only available to local authorities and authorised persons and they may only be made when notice has been given to those affected. They may be appealed against and may only last for up to 7 days. They do not involve the child being kept away from home, unless the court so directs. In contrast, emergency protection orders may be sought by anyone and are generally made without notice; there is no right of appeal, and provision for challenge is restricted to after 72 hours. They may only last for up to eight days unless specifically extended and the purpose of the order (when it is made at least) is to confer the right to remove the child from where he is. The applicant obtains parental responsibility for the child, whereas a child assessment order only deals with the issue of an assessment.

6.45 Now that a choice of two orders exists there may be a danger that the softer option of a child assessment order will be sought in borderline cases. Therefore, the court is given power to treat an application for such an order as an application for an *emergency protection order* and may not make a child assessment order if there are grounds to make an emergency protection order and it thinks that the latter is more appropriate in the child's interests [*section 43(4)*]. Of course, an emergency protection order may only be made where the court is satisfied that one of the conditions for such an order are satisfied.

6.46 Additionally, a child assessment order should be contrasted with an interim care or supervision order which may also deal with assessment issues. These orders may only be made following an application for a care or supervision order (*paragraphs 3.58–3.64*), and also where the court directs a local authority investigation under section 37 (*see paragraph 3.76*). Before either can be made, the court must be satisfied that there is reasonable cause to believe that the conditions for a full care or supervision order are fulfilled. Since these require evidence that the child is suffering or is likely to suffer significant harm, interim care and supervision orders will not be available in some cases in which a child assessment order could be made. An authority which have some evidence that a child is suffering or is likely to suffer significant harm but are uncertain about whether this evidence is correct might prefer to apply for a child assessment order, especially if they expect in the end to be able to leave the child safely at home without an order. If they have sufficient evidence and are looking for a care or supervision order, they will start proceedings directly for a care or supervision order.

RECOVERY ORDERS

6.47 Under the old law, where a child who was under a care or place of safety order was abducted or ran away from the person responsible for him, he might be arrested or, if he could not be found, a summons to produce the child or a search warrant might be issued [*section 16 of the Child Care Act 1980 and section 32 of the Children and Young Persons Act 1969*]. These powers reflected that a care order could be used as a sentence for a juvenile offender. They are replaced by the right to apply for a recovery order, which may be made to assist the recovery of a child who is in care, under an emergency protection order or in police protection [*section 50(2)*]. Such an order may be applied for by the person who has parental responsibility for the child by virtue of the care or emergency order or, in the case of police protection, by the designated officer [*section 50(4)*].

6.48 A recovery order may be made where there is reason to believe that the child:

(a) has been unlawfully taken away or is being unlawfully kept away from a person who for the time being has care of him by virtue of the care or emergency order or police protection ('the responsible person'). This phrase means any person who for the time being has care of him by virtue of the care or emergency order or police protection, such as a foster parent or a person running a children's home [*sections 49(2) and 50(2)*];

(b) has run away or is staying away from the responsible person, or

(c) is missing [*section 50(1)*].

6.49 The effect of a recovery order is to:

(a) direct a person who is in a position to do so to produce the child on request to an authorised person;

(b) authorise the removal of the child by an authorised person [*obstruction of the power of removal may be an offence: section 50(9)*];

(c) authorise a constable to enter premises specified in the order and search for the child, using reasonable force if necessary. [*Premises may only be specified where there are reasonable grounds for believing the child to be on them: section 50(6).*];

(d) require any person who has information as to the child's whereabouts to disclose that information, if asked to do so, to a constable or an officer of the court (such as the Tipstaff in the High Court). A person may not refuse to comply with a request to disclose information on the grounds of incrimination [*section 50(3) and (11)*]. (*For the privilege against incrimination, see paragraph 8.23*).

The 'authorised person' referred to in (a) and (b) is a constable, a person specified by the court (such as the Tipstaff) and any person who is authorised by the person with parental responsibility for the child under the care or emergency protection order [*section 50(7). Where a person is authorised by a person with parental responsibility, he must produce a document of authority, if asked to do so: section 50(8)*].

6.50 Recovery orders may be made by a court in England, Wales or Northern Ireland [*section 50(14)*]. They may be enforced in Scotland as if they had been made by the Court of Session there [*section 50(13)*]. Steps are being taken to ensure that they will also be enforceable in the Isle of Man and Channel Islands [*in part by virtue of regulations under section 101.*] Where a child who is being looked after by a local authority is placed under a recovery order, the reasonable expenses of his recovery under the order may be charged to that authority [*section 50(12)*].

ABDUCTION OF CHILDREN

6.51 Where a child is in care, under an emergency protection order or in police protection, it is an offence for a person, knowingly and without reasonable excuse, to:

(a) take or keep the child away from the responsible person ('*responsible person' has the same meaning as in paragraph 6.48(a)*) [*section 49(2)*];

(b) induce, assist or incite the child to run away or stay away from the responsible person [*section 43(1) and (2)*].

6.52 This offence replaces the offences in the Child Care Act 1980 [*Part II of that Act.*]. Additional offences may also be committed under the Child Abduction Act 1984 and the common law (for example kidnapping).

6.53 The Children Act also ensures that a person who provides a refuge for a child who is at risk of harm will not be criminally liable for an offence of abduction [*under the Act or the Child Abduction Act 1984 and certain other child care offences section 51(7)*] so long as certain conditions are observed. Immunity is given to those who provide a refuge in a voluntary or registered children's home (or as a local authority or voluntary organisation foster parent) where a certificate issued by the Secretary of State is in force [*section 51(5) and (6)*]. Regulations will set out the requirements which must be complied with while a certificate is in force and for the withdrawal of certificates in certain circumstances. The intention is to permit so-called 'safehouses' which operate as refuges for children who run or stay away from home to be free from potential prosecution, provided they act in accordance with the regulations. One of these requirements will be that the person running the refuge must notify the police of the reception of a child.

6.54 Paragraph 6.22 above referred to the power to issue a search warrant to support an emergency protection order. A search warrant may also be issued to assist a person who is exercising other powers of entry and inspection [*section 102(6)*]. The powers in question are those:

(a) of a supervisor to visit the supervised child and to have reasonable contact with him (*paragraphs 3.100–3.101*);

(b) of a person authorised by a local authority to enter and inspect a voluntary home, a children's home, premises in which a privately fostered child is believed to be accommodated, premises in which child minding or day care is believed to be provided, or an independent school, a residential care home, a nursing home or a mental nursing home in which children are accommodated so as to impose duties under the Act [*chapter 7*];

(c) of a person authorised by the Secretary of State to enter and inspect premises (*under the power mentioned in paragraph 8.16*);

(d) of a person authorised by a local authority to visit a child who is 'protected' under adoption legislation [*Adoption Act 1976, section 33*].

6.55 The condition which must be satisfied before a warrant may be issued is that a person has been prevented, or is likely to be prevented, from exercising his powers by being refused entry to the premises concerned or refused access to the child concerned [*section 102(1)*]. The search warrant authorises a constable to assist that person in the exercise of his powers, using reasonable force if necessary. Both the application for the warrant and the warrant itself should name the child, or describe him as clearly as possible, if it relates to a particular child and it is reasonably practicable to do so [*section 102(5)*]. In executing the warrant, the constable must be accompanied by the applicant if the latter so desires and the court does not otherwise direct [*section 102(2)*]. The court may also direct that the constable may be accompanied by a registered medical practitioner, a registered nurse or a registered health visitor if he so chooses [*section 102(3)*].

TRANSITIONAL PROVISIONS

6.56 Where a place of safety order was in force at the time of implementation of the Act, it continues to have effect as if the Act had not been passed. The only exception to this is that the power to apply for an 'interim order' to continue to hold onto the child is repealed [*Schedule 14, paragraph 27*]. Steps must be taken under the Act itself if authority is needed to hold onto the child once the place of safety order has run its course.

6.57 Similarly, the implementation of the Act does not affect a summons or warrant issued to recover a child who is in care or under a place of safety order [*Schedule 14, paragraphs 28 and 29*].

CHAPTER 7   <u>WELFARE OF CHILDREN AWAY FROM HOME</u>

7.1 This chapter outlines the protection which is afforded to children who are looked after away from home, other than by local authorities. The Act identifies a number of arrangements which may be made for children and which require regulation. The first of these arises where children spend time in day care or with a child minder. Also covered are children who go to live with a private foster parent and those who are accommodated in a children's home, by a voluntary organisation, in a hospital, a residential care home, a nursing or mental nursing home or an independent school, or by a local education authority.

7.2 In each case the scheme of the Act is similar. Those providing the facility in question must be registered or must give notification of the reception of children. In most cases the local authority is under a general duty to take steps to satisfy themselves as to the welfare of the children concerned. Requirements may be imposed on the providers and, where necessary, they may be prevented from looking after children. (*There is no power to prevent a local education authority or hospital from accommodating children, although court orders for the protection of children will always be available, see Chapters 3 and 6*).

CHILD MINDING AND DAY CARE

7.3 Part X of the Act modifies and updates the Nurseries and Child Minders Regulation Act 1948, which is repealed. Like that Act, this Part also applies in Scotland. Registration duties are simplified with the intention of making their enforcement more effective. Local authorities now must keep a single register of the persons who:

(a) act as child minders on domestic premises in their area; or

(b) provide day care on non-domestic premises in their area [*section 71(1)*].

In both cases people only have to be registered if there are children concerned who are under eight and are looked after for a period which exceeds two hours (or for periods which add up to more than two hours in any day) [*section 71(1) and (2)*]. Separate registration is required of persons in respect of day care which is provided on different premises in an authority's area [*section 71(3)*]. The register must be open to public inspection [*section 71(15)*].

7.4 A child minder is a person who looks after children who are under eight for reward [*section 71(2)(a)*]. Certain people are excluded from the definition of a child minder. These are the child's parents and relatives, any other person who has parental responsibility for him and a foster parent of the child [*section 71(4)*]. Also, the child's nanny is not a child minder while she looks after the child wholly or mainly in the home of the person who employs her as a nanny [*section 71(5)*]. Someone who works as a nanny for two people is also exempt while looking after any of the children wholly or mainly in the home of either of her employers (*section 71(6)*). By 'a nanny' is meant a person who is employed to look after the child by a parent, any other person who has parental responsibility for the child or a relative who has assumed for his care [*section 71(13)*]. These rules will exclude most babysitters from the controls of Part X.

7.5 People do not need to be registered in respect of child minding or day care if the children concerned are being looked after in a school (except in respect of an independent nursery school which operates as a day nursery) as part of the school's activities. [*Schedule 9 paragraph 3*]. Persons need not be registered in respect of day care where children are looked after in certain homes and hospitals [*and it is provided as part of the establishment's activities by the person who carries on the home or hospital or an authorised employee, Schedule 9, paragraph 4*]. These exemptions are similar to those under the old law. They do not apply if the premises are used to provide day care or child minding by an outside agent (ie. someone who neither runs the establishment in question nor is an authorised employee). There is a new exemption from registration in favour of occasional facilities such as crèches. If day care is provided on particular premises for less than six days a year, registration is not required provided that the local authority are notified in writing before the first time the premises are used in that year [*Schedule 9, paragraph 5*].

7.6 Applications for registration will have to contain a statement about the applicant and those who are likely to look after children or live on the premises in question [*Schedule 9, paragraph 1(1)*]. The local authority should check whether any of these people are disqualified from being registered. Disqualification arises if one of the circumstances prescribed in regulations apply to them (such as that they have committed certain offences or previously had registration cancelled) [*schedule 9, paragraph 2*]. Disqualification means that a person may not provide the service in question without the consent of the local authority. A fee will have to accompany the application to register [*schedule 9, paragraph 1(3)*].

7.7 A local authority may decline to register an applicant if any person who is likely to look after children, if the application is granted, is not fit to look after children who are under eight. Similarly, registration may be declined if a person who is likely to live or work at the premises in which the facility would be provided is not fit to be in the proximity of children who are under eight; or if the premises in which the facility would be carried on are not fit for children of that age [*section 71(7)–(11)*].

7.8 If registration is granted, a certificate must be issued. This certificate should specify any requirements which have been imposed on the applicant [*schedule 9, paragraph 6*]. Certain reasonable requirements must be imposed on the providers of day care and child minding. These include specification of the maximum number of children who may be looked after and a duty to notify the local authority of any change in the persons who look after children or live in the premises concerned. The local authority may impose other requirements if they see fit. Regulations may provide that certain requirements must, or must not, be imposed [*sections 72 and 73*].

7.9 A person authorised by the local authority may enter premises in which child minding is being carried on or day care is provided. He may inspect the premises, the children who are looked after, the arrangements for their welfare and any records which are kept relating to the service [*section 76(1)–(3)*]. Obstruction of the power of entry may be an offence [*section 76(7)*]. A warrant may be obtained to support the inspection powers (see paragraph 6.54). Inspections must be carried out at least once a year [*section 76(4)*]. A fee may be charged for the annual inspection [*schedule 9, paragraph 7*].

7.10 Registration may be cancelled on one of several grounds, namely that the circumstances which exist would entitle registration to be declined, the care which is provided is seriously inadequate for the needs of the children, a requirement has been broken or the annual fee is unpaid [*section 74(1)–(3)*]. Payment of the annual inspection fee is a condition of continued registration [*Schedule 9, paragraph 7(2)*]. In considering the needs of the children particular regard should be had to their religious persuasion, racial origin and cultural and linguistic background [*section 74(6)*].

7.11 Decisions of local authorities regarding registration and requirements may only be made after giving the applicant (or registered person) a chance to make representations [*section 77(1)–(4)*]. Appeals may be made to a court [*section 77(6)*]. Cancellation of registration (and imposition, removal or variation of requirements) only takes effect after there has been time for an appeal to be made [*section 77(11)*]. To permit immediate cancellation (or imposition, removal or variation of requirements), an alternative procedure is introduced by the Act. The local authority may apply directly to court for an order of cancellation (etc.) without giving notice to the registered person. The order may be made if one of the children who is provided with the service is suffering significant harm or is likely to do so [*section 75(1)–(3)*]. The order has immediate effect, although, as in the case of most orders under the Act, the registered person will be able to challenge it on appeal [*section 75(2) and 77(6)*].

7.12 Providers of day care who fail to register (without reasonable excuse) are liable to commit an offence [*section 78(1) and (2)*]. To protect the occasional child minder from criminal liability, she no longer commits an offence unless, having failed to register, the local authority serve an enforcement notice on her and, within a year of that notice, she acts as a child minder again (without reasonable excuse) [*section 78(3)–(7)*].

7.13 Local education authorities are placed under a new duty to assist a local authority which so requests with respect to their functions under Part X, provided that the assistance requested is compatible with their own obligations and does not unduly prejudice the discharge of their functions [*Schedule 9, paragraph 8A*].

7.14 Persons and premises registered under the Nurseries and Child-Minders Regulation Act 1948 at the time of implementation of Part X continue to come within that Act for twelve months or until registration is effected under Part X, if sooner [*Schedule 14, paragraphs 33 and 34*].

PRIVATE FOSTERING

7.15 Part IX of the Children Act replaces the Foster Children Act 1980. Local authority functions in respect of privately fostered children are similar to those under the 1980 Act. However, a number of changes have been made to come into line with local authority functions in respect of other children away from home. For example, the 'usual fostering limit' of three children will apply. Unless exemption from the limit has been granted by the local authority, the arrangement will be classed as a children's home. Secondly, the welfare duty which is now owed to privately fostered children is now the same as that owed to children living in children's homes and voluntary homes. Thirdly, the power to remove a foster child from his placement has been repealed, given that the emergency procedures described in Chapter 6 cover such children.

7.16 Generally speaking, private foster children are those whose parents place them for more than 28 days by private arrangement with a family which is not related to the child. Payment may be made by the parents but this is not necessary. Unlike under the 1980 Act, placements for less than a month will not be classed as private fostering, even if the person caring for the child is a 'regular foster parent'. In future shorter placements of children who are under eight which are made for reward will be 'child minding' (*paragraphs 7.3–7.5 above*). There is no concept of 'a regular foster parent'. To be 'privately fostered' the following conditions must be satisfied:

(a) the child is under sixteen [*section 66(1)*]. Or, in the case of a disabled child, is under eighteen [*section 66(4)*];

(b) he is cared for and accommodated by someone who is not his parent or a relative of his and has not got parental responsibility for him [*section 66(1)*];

(c) he has been cared for and accommodated by that person for at least 28 days (or for a shorter period if the intention is that he should stay that long) [*section 66(2)*];

(d) he is not looked after by a local authority (in which case a family placement will usually be with a 'local authority foster parent') or on behalf of a voluntary organisation [*Schedule 8, paragraph 1 and 2(c)*]. Placements by voluntary organisations are considered in paragraphs 7.35–7.39 below;

(e) he is not living in premises in which a parent, a person who has parental responsibility for him or a relative who has assumed responsibility for his care is living [*Schedule 8, paragraph 2(1) (a)*].

7.17 A child is not considered to be privately fostered in certain other circumstances, principally if he is living in a children's, voluntary or other home or institution (unless he is living there with someone who is caring for him in his personal capacity) [*Schedule 8, paragraphs 2–5*].

7.18 A proposal to foster a child privately must be notified to the local authority in whose area the fostering will take place. The detailed requirements of notification will be set down in regulations [*Schedule 8, paragraph 7*]. It is intended to require notification to be given by the putative foster parent and any other person who is involved in the arrangement. A parent will have to notify if he knows of the arrangement even if he is not involved.

7.19 Local authorities are required to satisfy themselves that the welfare of privately fostered children in their area is being satisfactorily safeguarded and promoted. They must also secure that private foster parents are given advice, where it seems to be needed [*section 67(1)*]. Regulations will set out the circumstances in which local authorities should visit private foster children and how local authorities should carry out their functions in respect of these children [*section 67(2)*]. The authority may inspect premises in which private fostering is taking place, or is proposed to take place, and may also inspect the children in them [*section 67(3)*].

7.20 Requirements may be imposed on private foster parents, such as regarding the number of children who may be taken in and the arrangements which must be made for their care [*Schedule 7, paragraphs 2 and 4*]. The local authority may also prohibit a person from privately fostering (or from fostering a particular child or from fostering in particular premises). Prohibitions may be imposed if a person is not suitable to foster a child, the premises are not suitable for fostering or it would be prejudicial to the welfare of the child for him to be fostered by the person in the premises concerned [*section 69(1)–(3)*]. Regulations will also specify the circumstances in which a person is disqualified from privately fostering a child without the consent of the local authority [*section 68*].

7.21 If a local authority are not satisfied about the welfare of a child who is privately fostered, they must consider whether they should exercise any of their functions under the Act [*section 67(5)*]. They may decide to impose requirements or even a prohibition on the foster parent. The investigation duties described in paragraphs 6.3 to 6.9 may be triggered. If they need to remove the child, they may consider applying for a emergency protection order or a care order. Unless it would not be in the best interests of the child concerned, they must take reasonable steps to secure that the child is looked after by a parent or relative of his or someone else who has got parental responsibility for him [*section 67(5)*].

7.22 Where the local authority make a decision about a requirement, prohibition or a disqualified person, an appeal may be made to the court within 14 days of notification of that decision [*Schedule 8, paragraph 8*]. Failure to notify the local authority of private fostering arrangements, breaches of requirements, prohibitions and disqualifications, and obstruction of powers of entry may be criminal offences [*section 70*]. A search warrant is available to support the power of entry (*paragraph 6.54*).

7.23 Local authorities are given new responsibilities towards privately fostered children who have left their foster home. A person who is under 21 and who was (but is no longer) privately fostered at any time after his sixteenth birthday 'qualifies for advice and assistance' from the local authority in whose area he is [*section 24(2)*]. Only a disabled foster child may be so qualified (*see paragraph 7.16 above*). The local authority may (but is not required to) advise, assist and befriend such a person if he asks them for help which they can give, he seems to need advice and to be befriended, and his foster parents do not have the necessary facilities to advise or befriend him [*section 24(4)–(6)*]. Assistance may be in kind or, in exceptional circumstances, in cash. [*section 24(7)*]. It may also be conditional on repayment, except where a person is in receipt of income support or family credit, [*section 24(10)*]. If the person who has been advised or befriended lives in another authority's area (or proposes to live there), the local authority must inform that other local authority [*section 24(11)*].

REGISTERED CHILDREN'S HOMES

7.24 A 'children's home' is a home [*including an institution, section 63(9)*] which provides care and accommodation wholly or mainly for more than three children [*section 63(3)*]. These homes must be registered with the local authority under Part VIII of the Act [*section 63(1)*] which replaces the Children's Homes Act 1982 (which was never brought into force). They are essentially private sector homes which are run on a profit-making basis. Thus, community homes, voluntary homes and institutions which provide special services such as hospitals, nursing homes, residential care homes and schools are excluded from the definition of a children's home [*section 63(5)*]. The only exception is that an independent school which provides accommodation for not more than fifty children is a children's home [*section 63(6), unless it is approved by the Secretary of State under section 11(3)(a) of the Education Act 1981. The Secretary of State may exempt other homes from Part VIII, section 63(3)*].

7.25 A home is only a 'children's home' if more than three children are cared for and accommodated there (except that an independent school may be a children's home even though it provides accommodation for less than three children). A home does not cease to be such simply because numbers of children may drop: it is a children's home if it usually provides or is intended to provide care and accommodation for more than three children [*section 63(3)*]. To exclude what are more like domestic arrangements, a home is not a children's home if the children concerned are all siblings of each other [*section 63(12) and Schedule 7*]. Where there are less than four children in a home or the children are all siblings of each other, the arrangement will constitute fostering, if the other requirements are satisfied. (These are the requirements for local authority fostering, for private fostering and for placements with foster parents by voluntary organisations). Also to exclude domestic arrangements, a child does not count as a child in a children's home if either:

(a) he is cared for and accommodated by a parent or relative or another person who has parental responsibility for him; or

(b) a parent or a person with parental responsibility for him is living at the home; or

(c) the person caring for him is doing so in his personal capacity and not as part of his duties in relation to the home [*section 63(4) and (7). In the case of (c), the arrangement again may be fostering*].

7.26 The final qualification to the 'three children rule' is that even though there are more than three children in a home, the local authority may decide to treat a person as fostering rather than as carrying on a children's home. (The fostering will be local authority, private or provided by a voluntary organisation, depending on the circumstances.). Three children (who are not all siblings of each other) are 'the usual fostering limit' [*Schedule 7, paragraphs 2 and 3*]. In deciding whether to exempt a person from the usual fostering limit, a local authority will consider whether the nature of the proposed arrangement is more akin to fostering than a children's home and whether their powers and duties with respect to fostered children are adequate in the case in question. They must consider in particular how many children are proposed to be fostered and for how long; what arrangements will be made for the care and accommodation of the children; the likely and intended relationship between the children and the person concerned, and whether the welfare of children living in the accommodation will be safeguarded and promoted [*Schedule 7, paragraph 4*].

7.27 Exemption from the usual fostering limit is by way of a notice which may contain conditions and must name the children involved [*Schedule 7, paragraph 4(3)*]. If it is intended to take in a different child, further exemption is necessary. Exemption may be cancelled at any time [*Schedule 7, paragraph 4(4)*]. If it is cancelled, or if the person fosters a child who is not named in the exemption notice, he is treated as carrying on a children's home and not as a foster parent [*Schedule 7, paragraph 5*]. He is then required to register the children's home. Decisions regarding exemption may be appealed against by a private foster parent [*Schedule 8, paragraph 8(1)*]. For all types of foster parent, the local authority must establish a procedure to consider representations (including complaints) about such decisions [*Schedule 7, paragraph 6*].

7.28 Where a child was a foster child under the Foster Children Act 1980 at the time Part VIII of the Children Act came into force and the circumstances are such that, unless exempted, registration as a children's home would be required, for three months after implementation the controls relating to private fostering will apply rather than those under Part VIII (children's homes). Part VIII will bite three months after implementation (so that non-registration as a children's home is an offence) unless an application to so register has been made in that time and has not been refused [*Schedule 14, paragraph 32*] or the arrangement has been exempted by the local authority from the controls of that Part.

7.29 Regulations will set out the registration procedure for children's homes and the kinds of requirements which must be satisfied before an application may be granted [*Schedule 6, paragraph 1*]. The local authority will be able to impose conditions on the applicant with respect to the home [*Schedule 6, paragraph 2*]. Registration must be reviewed annually and may be cancelled at any time if the home is not being carried on in accordance with the relevant requirements [*Schedule 6, paragraphs 3 and 4*]. The local authority must give the applicant a chance to make representations before decisions are made about registration or conditions attaching to it [*Schedule 6, paragraphs 5–7*]. Appeals may be made to a Registered Homes Tribunal [*Schedule 6, paragraph 8*].

7.30 Where a person would be disqualified from privately fostering a child under the regulations mentioned in paragraph 7.20 above, he may not carry on or be involved in a children's home unless he has the consent of the local authority [*section 65(1)*]. A disqualified person may also not be employed in a children's home without consent [*section 65(2)*]. An appeal against refusal of consent may be made to a Registered Homes Tribunal [*Schedule 6, paragraph 8*].

7.31 Regulations will also be made governing the placement of children in children's homes, the conduct of such homes and the welfare of children living there [*Schedule 6, paragraph 10*].

7.32 The Act imposes welfare duties on the person carrying on the home which are similar to those which apply to local authorities in respect of children whom they look after. These duties are to safeguard and promote the welfare of a child accommodated in the home; to make reasonable use of the services and facilities which are available for children who are cared for by their own parents; and to advise, assist and befriend the child with a view to promoting his welfare when he ceases to be accommodated in the home [*section 64(1)*]. The person carrying on the home is also required to ascertain (so far as is reasonably practicable) and take into account the wishes and feelings of the child, his parents and other relevant people regarding decisions made about the child [*section 64(2) and (3)*]. The child's religious persuasion, racial origin and cultural and linguistic background should also be given due consideration [*section 64(3)*].

7.33 Duties are also imposed on local authorities [*section 64(4), which extends the application of section 62 to children's homes*]. They must satisfy themselves that the person carrying on a children's home in their area (or outside their area if a child is being accommodated in it on the authority's behalf) is satisfactorily safeguarding and promoting the welfare of children in the home. This is the same duty as is owed to private foster children in the local authority's area. Children in children's homes in the local authority's area must be visited from time to time, in the interests of their welfare. A person authorised by the local authority has a power of entry and inspection of the home; and he may inspect the children in the home and any records which must be kept under the regulations. If the authority are not satisfied about the welfare of a child in the home, then, as in the case of private fostering, they must consider whether to exercise their functions under the Act and must take reasonable steps to secure that he returns to a parent, a relative or another person who has parental responsibility for him.

7.34 Also as in the case of private fostering, regulations will be able to prescribe how local authorities carry out their general duties towards children who are living in children's homes, in particular the circumstances in which visiting is required [*section 62(3), as extended by section 64(4)*]. A person who is under twenty one and who left a registered children's home after his sixteenth birthday (but while still a child) qualifies for advice and assistance from his local authority (subject to the conditions in paragraph 7.23 above) [*section 24(2)*]. There is an additional duty in the case of a child from a registered children's home: if he leaves the home after his sixteenth birthday the person carrying on the home must inform the local authority for the area in which he proposes to live [*section 24(12)*].

VOLUNTARY HOMES AND VOLUNTARY ORGANISATIONS

7.35 A voluntary organisation is a body (other than a public or local authority) whose activities are not carried on for profit [*section 105(1)*]. When they accommodate children, they do so chiefly in voluntary homes and community homes or by placing them with foster parents. The Act updates the provisions of the Child Care Act 1980 which applied to these placements. Under that Act, children were said to be 'in the care of a voluntary organisation'. To avoid confusion, the word 'care' is not used by the Children Act in this context: instead children are referred to as provided with accommodation by the organisation.

7.36 A voluntary home is defined as a home or other institution providing care and accommodation for children which is carried on by a voluntary organisation [*section 60(3)*]. It does not include a hospital, a school, a residential care home, a nursing home or certain other homes [*section 60(3)*]. Unlike a children's home, a voluntary home is registered with the Secretary of State [*section 60(1)*]. Regulations will govern the placement of children in voluntary homes, the conduct of the homes and the welfare of children living there [*Schedule 5, paragraph 7*].

7.37 Where a voluntary organisation places a child with foster parents, the placement will be governed by regulation-making powers which are equivalent to those which apply to local authorities when they use foster parents [*section 59(2)*]. If a voluntary organisation places a child on behalf of a local authority, the child is treated as placed with local authority foster parents [*section 23(2)(a)*]. An important change from the old law is that the 'usual fostering limit' applies to voluntary organisations, so that placements of more than three children who are not all siblings of each other will be treated as a placement in a children's home if the local authority do not exempt it (*paragraph 7.26 above*).

7.38 Other placements of children by voluntary organisations will also be capable of regulation by the Secretary of State [*section 59(1)*]. Wherever the children are placed (return of a child to a parent or another person with parental responsibility for him is not considered to be a 'placement'), the general duties of the voluntary organisation are the same [*section 61*]. These duties, and the functions of local authorities towards children who are accommodated by voluntary organisations, are exactly the same as those which apply to a person who carries on a registered children's home. Regulations will provide that certain persons are disqualified from involvement in voluntary homes without consent [*Schedule 5,* paragraph 8]. Paragraphs 7.32–7.34 above are equally applicable to voluntary organisations. The only difference is that where a person qualifies for advice and assistance as a result of leaving accommodation provided by a voluntary organisation, the local authority are required (rather than empowered) to advise and befriend him if the conditions set out in paragraph 7.23 above are fulfilled [*section 24(4)*]. They are also empowered to assist the person concerned, [*section 24(6)*]. The duties which are imposed by the Act and which will be laid down in regulations represent a substantial improvement on the provision made in the Child Care Act 1980.

7.39 A further change is that a voluntary organisation will not be able to ask a local authority to pass a resolution vesting in them parental rights and duties with respect to a child whom they are looking after [*section 64 of the Child Care Act 1980*]. This power has been rarely used. Any existing resolutions will be brought to an end six months after the Act comes into force [*Schedule 14, paragraph 31*]. Where an organisation needs to ensure that a child will not be removed from accommodation which they have provided, they may seek a section 8 order (either with or without leave). The provisions which empowered voluntary organisations to arrange for children to emigrate are not repeated [*section 63 of the Child Care Act 1980*]. In future they will be subject to the general law regarding removal of children [*removal without the requisite consents may be an offence under the Child Abduction Act 1984, for example. For amendments to that Act, see Schedule 12 paragraph 37 and Schedule 15*].

CHILDREN ACCOMMODATED BY HEALTH OR LOCAL EDUCATION AUTHORITIES

7.40 A new duty is imposed on health and local education authorities which provide accommodation for a child for a consecutive period of more than three months [*this three month period does not include time before the Act was implemented: Schedule 14, paragraph 35*]. If a child is accommodated for that long, or if it is intended by the authority that he should be, the responsible local authority must be notified by the accommodating authority [*section 85(1)*]. The responsible local authority will be the authority for the area in which the child usually lives or, if there is no such authority, the authority in whose area the accommodation is situated [*section 85(3)*]. That authority must also be informed when the child leaves the accommodation which has been provided [*section 85(2)*].

7.41 When they have been notified, the responsible local authority must take reasonably practicable steps to enable them to decide whether the child's welfare is adequately safeguarded and promoted while he stays in the accommodation [*section 85(4)*]. They must also consider whether they should exercise any of their functions under the Act with respect to the child. In particular, they might decide to provide services to the child under Part III to promote contact between the child and his family. If a person who is under twenty one leaves accommodation which has been provided by a health or local education authority for at least three months, he may qualify for advice and assistance from the local authority in whose area he is. He will qualify provided that he was over sixteen (but still a child) when he left and the other conditions mentioned in paragraph 7.23 above are fulfilled [*section 24(4), which imposes a power rather than a duty to advise and assist*]. The health or local education authority must inform the local authority for the area in which the child proposes to live if a child who has reached sixteen leaves accommodation which has been provided for at least three months [*section 24(2). This duty is additional to that in section 85(2)*].

CHILDREN ACCOMMODATED IN RESIDENTIAL CARE, NURSING AND MENTAL NURSING HOMES

7.42 Residential care homes, mental nursing homes and nursing homes provide personal care for adults and children. Most such homes are registered and regulated under the Registered Homes Act 1984. The person carrying on one of these homes must notify the local authority if a child is accommodated either for three months consecutively, or with the intention (of the person who decides to accommodate him) that he should stay that long [*section 86(1)*]. The three month period does not include time before the Act was brought into force [*Schedule 14, paragraph 35*]. The local authority must also be informed when the child ceases to be so accommodated [*section 86(2)*]. The relevant local authority is the one in whose area the home is.

7.43 That authority has the same functions towards the child as were described in paragraph 7.41 above in respect of a child who has been accommodated by a health or local education authority. These functions are supported by a power to enter a residential care home, a mental nursing home or a nursing home in order to discover whether the duties in this and the preceding paragraph have been complied with [*section 86(5)*]. The person carrying on the home in question must inform the local authority for the area in which the child is going to live, if a child who has reached sixteen leaves the home after living there for three months. Such a child may qualify for advice and assistance from the local authority [*section 24(2)*] and (*paragraph 7.23 above*).

CHILDREN ACCOMMODATED IN INDEPENDENT SCHOOLS

7.44 The Children Act introduces a new duty on both the proprietor and the person responsible for the conduct of an independent school which accommodates a child to safeguard and promote the child's welfare [*section 87(1)*]. [*This duty does not apply to an independent school which is also a children's home or a residential care home. An independent school is defined as 'any school at which full-time education is provided for five or more pupils of compulsory school age (whether or not such education is also provided for pupils under or over that age), not being a school maintained by a local education authority, a grant-maintained school or a special school not maintained by a local education authority.' A proprietor in relation to any school, means 'the person or body of persons responsible for the management of the school . . . .' Education Act 1944, section 114(1)*]. As in the case of children accommodated by a local education authority and in residential care homes, the local authority for the area in which the school is must take reasonably practicable steps to enable them to decide whether the child's welfare is adequately safeguarded and promoted in the school [*section 87(3)*]. If they consider that the child's welfare is not being safeguarded and promoted, the authority must notify the Secretary of State [*section 87(4)*]. His powers are set out in sections 71–75 of the Education Act 1944.

7.45 A person authorised by the local authority may enter the school to enable the authority's welfare duty to be met [*section 87(5)*]. He may (subject to regulations) inspect the premises, the children and records which are kept by the school [*section 87(6)*].

7.46 Additional controls are provided where an independent school accommodates a pupil who is under 16 for more than two weeks during school holidays. A person who proposes to care for and accommodate a child in these circumstances must give written notice to the local authority (unless he is exempted by them); the child is treated as a privately fostered child, and the local authority's functions in Part IX apply [*Schedule 8, paragraph 9, with the exception that the local authority may not impose requirements under paragraph 6 of that Schedule*]. Notice must also be given to the local authority when a child ceases to be treated as a privately fostered child under these provisions.

RESIDENTIAL HOLIDAYS

7.47 No special provision is made in the Act for the regulation of residential holidays for children. Where care and accommodation is provided for children, these holidays will probably come within the regulations governing children's homes or voluntary homes. In appropriate cases, the Secretary of State will be able to exempt residential holidays from the regulations [*sections 60(3)(f) and 63(3)(b)*].

CHAPTER 8   ADOPTION, EVIDENCE, PROCEDURE AND OTHER MATTERS

8.1 This chapter highlights a number of additional areas of child law which are affected by the Act, including adoption, consent to marriage, juvenile offenders, the powers of the Secretary of State, evidence and procedural matters.

ADOPTION

8.2 The Government has set in motion a review of adoption law. In the meantime, the Children Act has led to a substantial number of amendments to adoption legislation, most of which are found in Schedule 10 of the Act [*some important repeals, such as of sections 14(3) and 15(4) of the Adoption Act 1976, are also found in Schedule 15*]. The chance has also been taken to clarify parts of the Adoption Act 1976 and to effect a small number of relatively straightforward improvements. The main changes are as follows.

8.3 Proceedings under the 1976 Act are 'family proceedings' and, therefore, a section 8 order may be made at any time during them. The court will decide whether to make a section 8 order by applying rules in Parts I and II of the Children Act, (*paragraphs 3.5–3.7, and Chapter 3 generally*). The relatively restrictive provisions introduced by the Children Act 1975 to encourage the making of custody rather than adoption orders in certain circumstances are not repeated [*as interpreted by the courts these provisions seemed to add little to the duty to do what is best for the child: Law Commission Report No. 172: Guardianship and Custody (1988), paragraph 4.36*].

8.4 If, in adoption proceedings, the court considers that it may be appropriate to make a care or supervision order, it may direct the local authority to investigate the child's circumstances. The authority will be able to apply for an order under Part IV of the Act. However, it will no longer be open to the court make a care or supervision order of its own motion 'in exceptional circumstances' (paragraphs 3.76–3.79).

8.5 It was explained in Chapter 5 that children are no longer treated as in the 'voluntary care' of a local authority (*paragraphs 5.2–5.7*). Instead, arrangements may be made for a child to be accommodated by a local authority or on their behalf. Unlike voluntary care, these arrangements may always be brought to an end at any time. Similarly, children are no longer 'in the care of' a voluntary organisation (*paragraph 7.35*). These changes have lead to a corresponding restriction of the right to apply to free a child for adoption. Under the old law, an application could be made without the consent of a parent or guardian if the child was 'in the care of' an adoption agency. This phrase was not defined in the 1976 Act but was taken to include a child in voluntary care. In future, however, an adoption agency will not be able to apply for a freeing order without the consent of a parent or guardian unless the agency is a local authority in whose care the child is (under a care order). [*Schedule 10, paragraphs 6(1) and 30(9), which insert sections 18(2A) and 72(1B) into the 1976 Act*]. It is not expected that this will cause a major change in practice, since an application for freeing without consent is unlikely while a child is accommodated on a voluntary basis.

8.6 The Registrar General is required to set up an Adoption Contact Register to enable adopted people to contact their birth parents and other relatives [*Schedule 10, paragraph 21, which inserts a new section 51A into the Adoption Act 1976*]. This register builds upon the informal contact service which the Registrar General has operated in recent years. It will only be open to people who are at least 18 years old. The Registrar General will pass on to an adopted person, who has registered with him, the name and address of a relative who has asked for his details to be placed on the register. In order to use the register, the people concerned will have to satisfy the Registrar of their identity and, in the case of the relative, of their relationship with the adopted person. A fee will also be charged. The address which either person supplies to the Registrar need not be of the place where he lives. An intermediary's address might be used where the person concerned preferred (for the time being at least) to contact the adopted person by letter rather than face-to-face or wanted to communicate his or her desire not to have further contact.

8.7 A further amendment to the 1976 Act assists people to obtain information about their birth records. A person who was adopted before 1975 is required to attend a counselling interview before he may be given information as to his birth records [Adoption Act 1976, section 51]. Under the present law the counselling interview has to take place in England, Wales or Scotland. The amendments permit counselling to be obtained either anywhere within the United Kingdom or from a body outside the United Kingdom which has notified the Registrar General that it is willing to provide counselling and satisfies the Registrar that it is suitable to do so [*schedule 10, paragraph 20, which amends section 51 of the 1976 Act*].

8.8 The Adoption Act and the Adoption (Scotland) Act 1978 are also amended to ensure that the work of adoption agencies (and court orders made) under the equivalent legislation in Northern Ireland are recognised [*Schedule 10, for example in paragraphs 2, 20, 30, 32, 41 and 46*].

8.9 In future, individual schemes for the payment of adoption allowances (to adopters and those who intend to adopt) will not need to be approved by the Secretary of State. Instead, they will be subject to regulations made by him. Existing schemes will be replaced by arrangements for payments made under the regulations. [*Schedule 10, paragraph 25, which inserts section 57A into the 1976 Act*].

CONSENT TO MARRIAGE

8.10 The Children Act substitutes in the Marriage Act 1949 a simpler and more coherent set of rules about whose consent is required to the marriage of a child who is 16 or 17 [*Schedule 12, paragraph 5, which amends the Marriage Act 1949*]. Unless there is a residence or a care order in force with respect to the child, the consent of each parent who has parental responsibility for the child and each guardian (if any) is needed [*the court has power to permit marriage in the face of parental opposition, section 3 of the 1949 Act*]. Where the child is subject to a residence order, only the consent of the person with whom he lives as a result of the order is required. In most cases a residence order will cease to have effect when the child reaches sixteen. Therefore, where that happens and the child has not since then been placed under a residence or care order which is still in force, only the consent of the person with whom the child was to live under that residence order is required. However, if a care order is in force, the consent of each person with parental responsibility for the child (including the local authority) is needed. [*a care order brings an existing residence order to an end, section 91(2). Where an old style custody order is in force, transitional provisions apply Schedule 14, paragraph 37*]

8.11 Care orders may no longer be imposed as a sentence in criminal proceedings [*section 7(7) (a) of the Children and Young Persons Act 1969 is repealed by Schedule 15*]. The fact that a child has committed an offence may be evidence that he is suffering or is likely to suffer significant harm so that a local authority may apply for a care or supervision order in respect of him (*paragraphs 3.48–3.57*). 'Harm' includes impairment of behavioural or social development [*section 31(9)*]. However, it is not to be open to the police to apply for such an order.

8.12 Supervision orders may still be made in criminal proceedings. In recent years these orders have become dissimilar to supervision orders which are made in care proceedings under the Children and Young Persons Act 1969. The differences between criminal and civil supervision orders increase under the Children Act. First, supervision orders under the Act may impose requirements on those with parental responsibility for the child and other people with whom the child is living (*paragraphs 3.100–3.103*). Secondly, the Act introduces a further requirement which may be imposed under a criminal supervision order: that the child or young person will live in accommodation provided by or on behalf of the local authority for up to six months ('a residence requirement') [*Schedule 12, paragraph 23, which inserts a new section 12AA into the 1969 Act*]. Such a requirement may also stipulate that the child or, in the terminology of the 1969 Act, 'young person', which term includes a child who is 14 or more, will not live with a named person during that period.

8.13 A residence requirement is intended to be available for a repeat offender who has committed a serious offence and whose criminal behaviour is attributable to the circumstances in which he is living [*section 12AA(5) of the 1969 Act*]. A residence requirement may not be imposed unless the child has been convicted of an offence which the court considers to be serious and which, if committed by a person over twenty one, would have been imprisonable. This offence must have been committed while there was in force an earlier supervision order (under the 1969 Act) which (i) imposed requirements under section 12A(3) of the 1969 Act or (ii) imposed a previous residence requirement under section 12AA of the same Act. Finally, except where the child was already subject to a residence requirement, his criminal behaviour must have been due, to a significant extent, to the circumstances in which he was living. A social inquiry report should usually have been obtained into the circumstances in which the child was living and the child should have had the chance to be legally represented before the requirement is imposed [*section 12AA(5)–(11)*].

8.14 Existing criminal care orders will come to an end six months after the Act comes into force [*Schedule 14, paragraph 36*]. Until that time, the old law will continue to apply to them, for example regarding the duration of the order and the right to apply for its discharge [*sections 15, 20 and 21 of the 1969 Act*]. The six month period is intended to give local authorities the chance to apply for a care or supervision order under the Act if that would be appropriate. Where a criminal care order is in force, the local authority are given an additional power to apply for an order that the child should live in accommodation provided by them for up to six months. This order has the effect of a supervision order with a residence requirement, even though the pre-conditions for such an order do not need to be satisfied.

8.15 The power to remand a child or young person to the care of a local authority is replaced by remand to accommodation provided by the local authority [*Schedule 12, paragraph 26, which inserts a new section 23 into the 1969 Act. For the position of children who are detained after arrest, see paragraph 53 of Schedule 13, which makes consequential amendments to section 38(6) of the Police and Criminal Evidence Act 1984*]. The intention is that a remanded child should no longer be treated as if he were under a care order. He will be 'looked after' by the local authority, who will not have parental responsibility for him, although it is expressly stated that a person acting on behalf of the authority may lawfully detain the remanded person [*section 23(3) of the 1969 Act, as amended by paragraph 26A of Schedule 12*].

THE FUNCTIONS OF THE SECRETARY OF STATE

8.16 Part XI of the Act updates and extends the functions of the Secretary of State in connection with children. These functions include the power to inspect premises in which children are accommodated and to inspect the children, the arrangements in the home and records which are kept there, to require people who provide services for children to supply him with information, to cause inquiries to be held and to conduct (or help others to conduct) research in matters related to children [*sections 80–83*]. Local authorities may also conduct or assist others to conduct research [*section 83(2)*].

8.17 The Act places the Secretary of State under a new duty to review the adequacy of the provision of child care training [*section 83(8)*]. 'Child care training' is defined in section 82(6). Such reviews will take on board representations made to him by the Central Council for Education and Training in Social Work, local authorities and others. The Secretary of State may make grants to people who undergo child care training [*section 82(1)*].

8.18 The Secretary of State is also given default powers where a local authority fails to comply with duties imposed on them under the Children Act. If the authority has so failed without reasonable excuse, the Secretary of State may make an order declaring the authority to be in default. This order may contain directions to the authority for compliance with their duties. These directions may be enforced in the High Court by an order of mandamus [*section 84*].

EVIDENCE AND PROCEDURAL MATTERS

Hearsay

8.19 The Children Act gives the Lord Chancellor power to provide by order for hearsay evidence to be admissible in civil proceedings relating to children. Such an order may only extend to evidence in connection with an issue relating to the upbringing, maintenance or welfare of a child. This power would enable the effect of the ruling against hearsay evidence in *Re H and Re K* [*1989 Family Law 296*] to be reversed.

Evidence of Young Children in Civil Proceedings

8.20 The Children Act enables a court to hear the unsworn evidence of a child in *any* civil proceedings [*section 96(1)–(2)*]. It may do so where, in the court's opinion, the child understands that it is his duty to speak the truth and has sufficient understanding to justify his evidence being heard. Previously, a court in civil proceedings could not hear the evidence of a child who did not understand the nature of an oath. In contrast, such a child's evidence has been admissible in criminal proceedings for a long time [*section 38 of the Children and Young Persons Act 1933*]. The result, for example, is that the evidence of a young child that he has been abused will be equally admissible in criminal proceedings against the alleged abuser, in proceedings under the Act regarding his welfare and any other civil proceedings such as wardship or tort.

Privacy in Magistrates' Courts

8.21 Rules which prevent the publication of details of children's cases which are heard in private in the High Court and county courts continue to have effect [*for example, section 12 of the Administration of Justice Act 1960, as amended by Schedule 13, paragraph 14*]. The Act enables rules of court to permit a magistrates' court to sit in private in proceedings in which powers under it may be exercised with respect to a child [*section 97(1)*]. The Act also creates a new of fence to prohibit the publication of material which is likely to identify a child as being involved in such proceedings in a magistrates' court [*including his address or school as being that of a child involved in such proceedings, section 97(2)*]. This offence covers radio and television broadcasts as well as printed material [*the offence is similar to that in section 49 of the Children and Young Persons Act 1933 regarding juvenile courts*].

8.22 An offence is not committed if it is proved that the accused did not know and had no reason to suspect that the publication was intended or likely to identify the child [*section 97(3)*]. If it is in the child's interests, the court or the Secretary of State may permit publication to go ahead which would identify the child [*section 97(4)*]. An example would be where publicity may help to trace a child who is missing.

The Privilege against Incrimination

8.23 The Act makes special provision for proceedings in respect of care, supervision, emergency protection, child assessment and other orders under Parts IV and V. These are proceedings which concern a child who may be at particular risk. Previously, a witness in equivalent proceedings under the Children and Young Persons Act 1969 might refuse to give evidence which would enable the court to decide what steps should be taken to protect the child concerned. He could do so on the ground that to give such evidence might incriminate him or his spouse of an offence. He would have been made aware that, if he gave such evidence in the child protection proceedings, it could then be used as evidence in criminal proceedings. In practice, a child protection case may have been deferred until the outcome of a criminal prosecution was known (and a conviction might have been important evidence in those later proceedings). In order to encourage witnesses to give evidence and to help avoid delay in children's cases, a person will no longer be able to refuse to give evidence or answer a question put to him while he gives evidence simply on the ground of incrimination [*section 98*]. His evidence and his answers will not then be admissible against the witness or his spouse in criminal proceedings (except perjury).

Attendance of the Child

8.24 The court in proceedings which relate to orders under Parts IV and V is also given power to order the child concerned to attend court. This order may be supported by an order authorising a constable or another specified person to bring the child to court; authorising entry and search of specified premises; requiring that a person who is in a position to do so should bring the child to court; and requiring a person to disclose information about the child's whereabouts [*section 95*]. These powers replace the duty to bring a child before the court in care proceedings. They would be useful where the court wishes to see the child who is the subject of proceedings but the person who is looking after him is unwilling to bring him to court.

Printed in the United Kingdom for HMSO
Dd.295187, 2/92, C50, 3390/3, 5673, 151961